SIGHT
WORDS

This book belongs to:

Tara

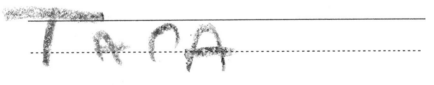

PRIMER
PRE-PRIMER

What's Inside

In this book you will find 92 sight words that are common in the English language based on the dolch sight word lists. All primer and pre-primer words are included with one multi-faceted activity page per word. After the first 10 words, flip back to where additional activities are included to help solidify the child's new knowledge for that set of words!

The repetitive nature of the activities is purposeful and fosters independent work as they learn what is expected of them with each sheet. This book is designed to give consistently similar activities for each word, providing repetition. Activities should be used as one part of a comprehensive reading and sight word curriculum.

Activities included: identifying, tracing, see & say, writing, and spelling as well as word searches, copying, and shape box writing. Perfect for ages 4-6 or anyone who needs extra practice with sight words.

Pre-Primer Sight Words:

a	find	is	not	three
and	for	it	one	to
away	funny	jump	play	two
bit	go	little	red	up
blue	help	look	run	we
can	here	make	said	where
come	I	me	see	yellow
down	in	my	the	you

Primer Sight Words:

all	came	into	please	that	went
am	did	like	pretty	there	what
are	do	must	ran	they	white
at	eat	new	ride	this	who
ate	four	no	saw	too	will
be	get	now	say	under	with
black	good	on	she	want	yes
brown	have	our	so	was	
but	he	out	soon	well	

a

Color the word.

Trace the word.

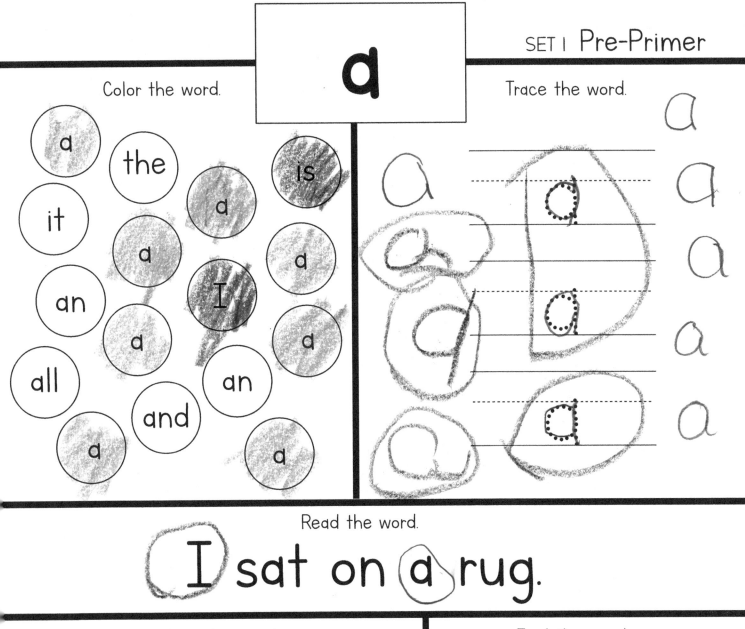

Read the word.

I sat on a rug.

Write the word.

I see a cat.

I see a bus.

I see a pig.

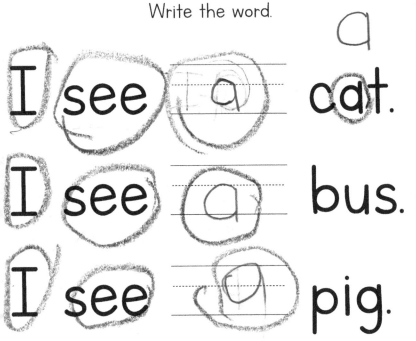

Find the word.

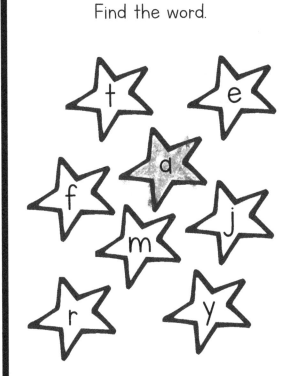

and

Color the word.

Trace the word.

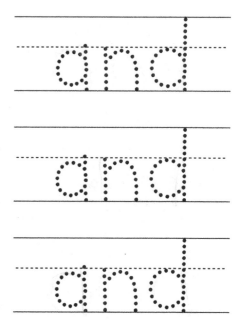

Read the word.

I play with the bat and ball.

Write the word.

I like my bear

and my book.

Spell the word.
< connect the letters >

away

Color the word.

Trace the word.

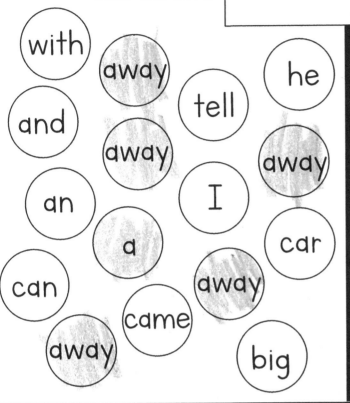

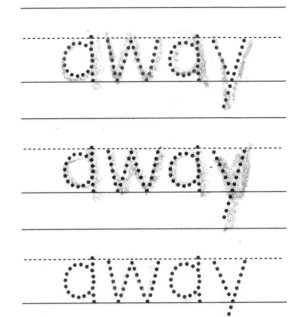

Read the word.

He went away.

Write the word.

The bus drove from school.

Spell the word.
< connect the letters >

big

Color the word.

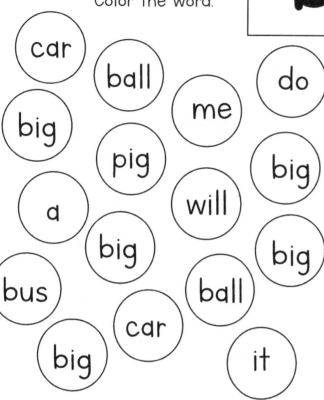

car
ball
do
big
me
pig
big
a
will
big
bus
big
ball
car
big
it

Trace the word.

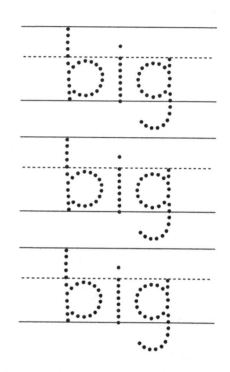

Read the word.

The bus is big.

Write the word.

I see a _____ dog.

Spell the word.
< connect the letters >

e
h
b
v
i
o
q
g

blue

Color the word.

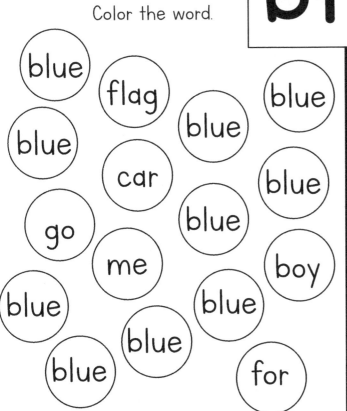

Trace the word.

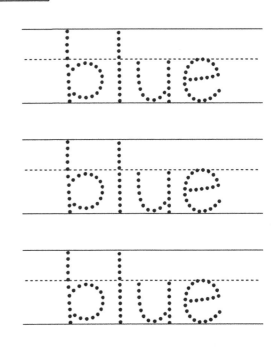

Read the word.

The hat is blue.

Write the word.

The _____ car went fast.

Spell the word.
< connect the letters >

can

Color the word.

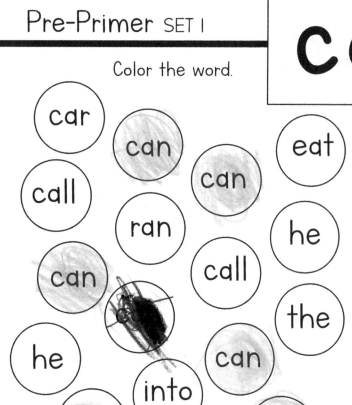

car | can | can | eat
call | ran | call | he
can | | the
he | into | can
can | can

Trace the word.

can

can

can

Read the word.

I can be kind.

Write the word.

She ___can___ help.

He ___can___ sing.

I ___can___ play.

Spell the word.
< connect the letters >

t   x
n
f   q
d
c   v

come

Color the word.

Trace the word.

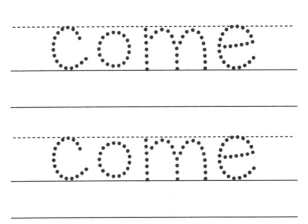

Read the word.

Come with me.

Write the word.

_____

Spell the word.
< connect the letters >

with me.

down

Color the word.

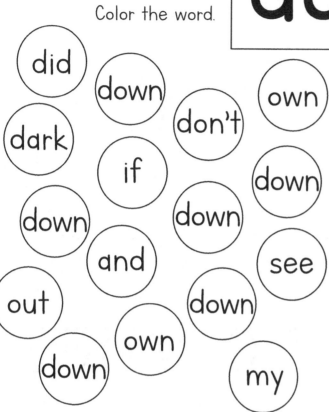

did
down
own
dark
don't
if
down
down
down
and
see
out
down
own
down
my

Trace the word.

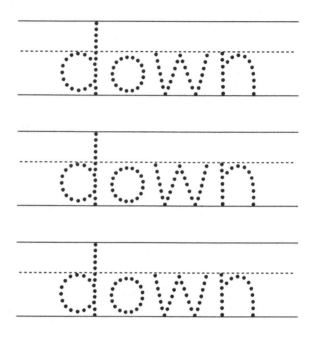

down
down
down

Read the word.

They sat down.

Write the word.

I sat _____ .

We sat _____ .

Sit _____ .

Spell the word.
< connect the letters >

t   e
h
f
n
o
d   w

find

Color the word.

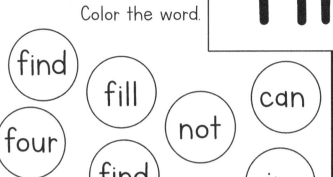
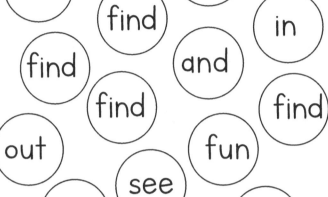

Trace the word.

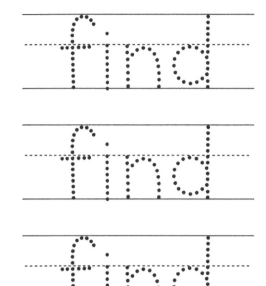

Read the word.

I will find my toy.

Write the word.

I can _____
the cat.

Spell the word.
< connect the letters >

for

Color the word.

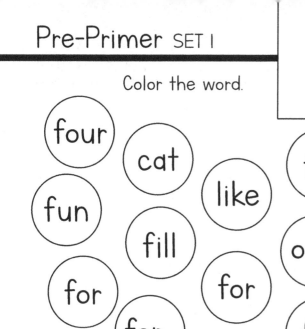
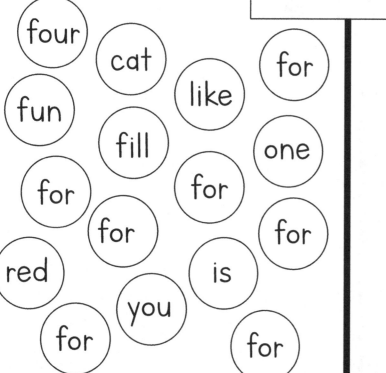

four
cat
like
for
fun
fill
one
for
for
for
red
is
for
you
for

Trace the word.

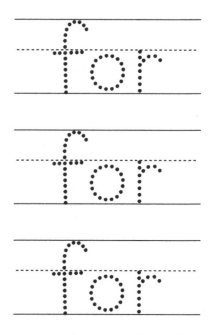

Read the word.

Wait for us.

Write the word.

The dog is _____ sale.

Spell the word.
< connect the letters >

t r o f f m r y

funny

Color the word.

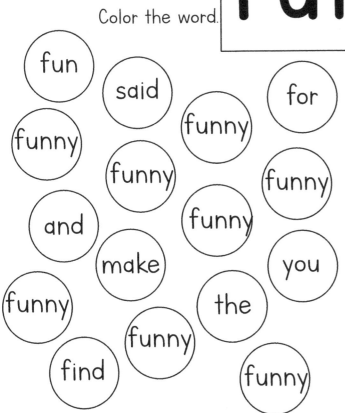

fun · said · funny · for · funny · funny · funny · and · make · funny · you · funny · the · find · funny · funny

Trace the word.

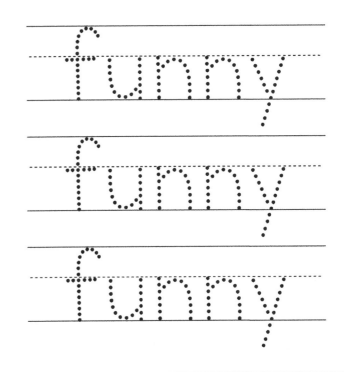

funny
funny
funny

Read the word.

I saw a funny book.

Write the word.

I see a picture.

Spell the word.
< connect the letters >

n · e · n · y · u · m · r · f

go

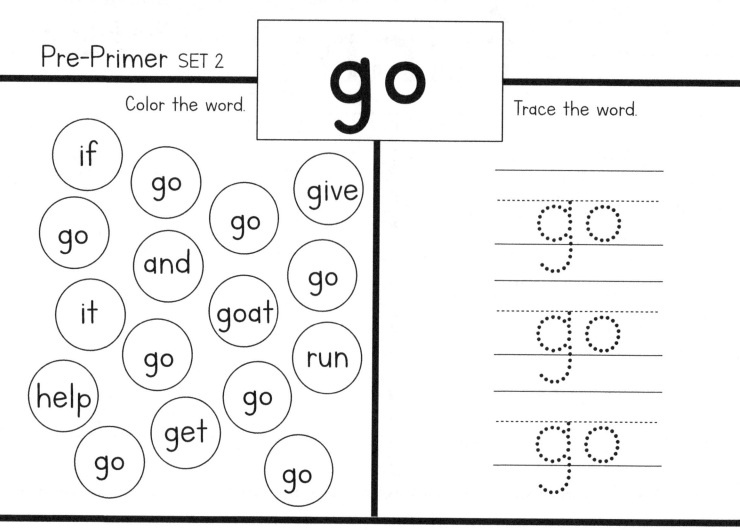

Color the word.

if, go, give, go, go, and, go, it, goat, go, go, run, help, go, get, go, go

Trace the word.

go
go
go

Read the word.

I will go to the store.

Write the word.

Green means

_____
_____ .

Spell the word.
< connect the letters >

u, g, o, s, d, a, y, l

help

Color the word.

help · have · him · help · help · help · want · on · help · has · help · here · say · help · ride

Trace the word.

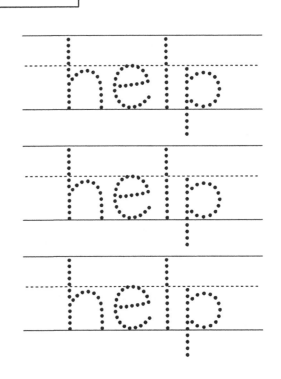

Read the word.

I like to help mom.

Write the word.

Please

me.

Spell the word.
< connect the letters >

here

Color the word.

Trace the word.

Read the word.

Please come here.

Write the word.

The bus will drive _____.

Spell the word.
< connect the letters >

I

Color the word.

Trace the word.

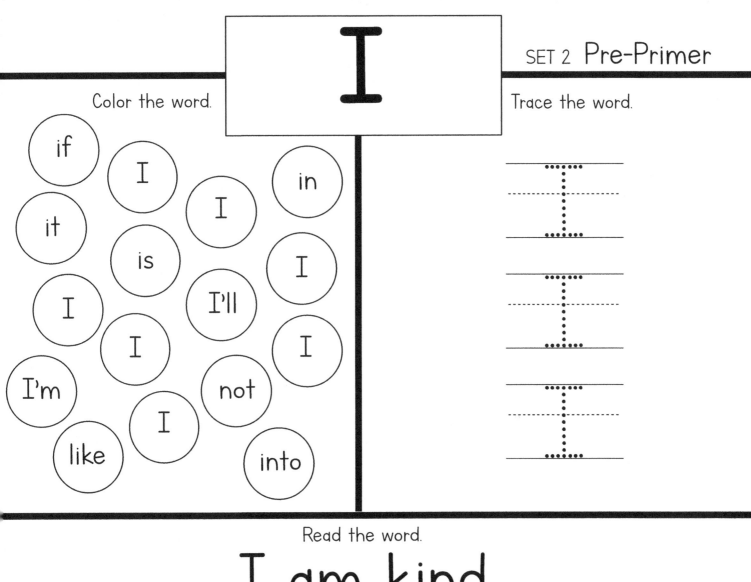

if I in
it I
is I
I I'll
I I
I'm not
I
like into

Read the word.

I am kind.

Write the word.

_____ will go.

_____ say hi.

_____ can help.

Spell the word.
< color the letter >

in

Color the word.

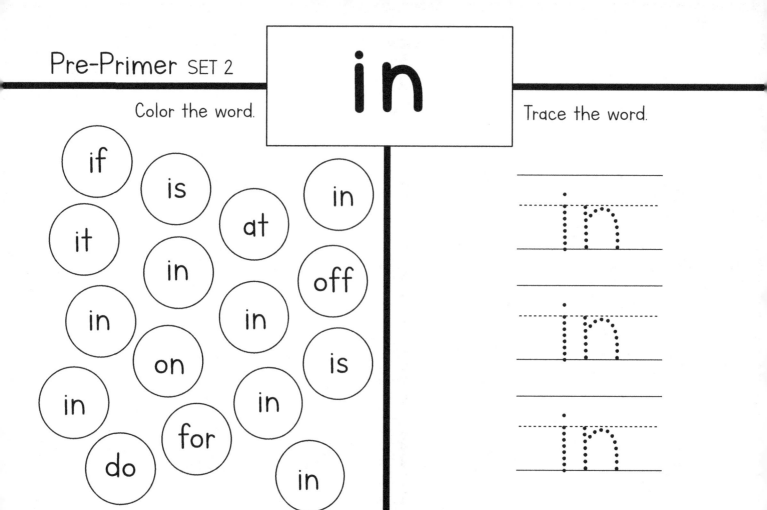

Trace the word.

Read the word.

I am in bed.

Write the word.

It is time to come _____.

Spell the word.
< connect the letters >

is

Color the word.

Trace the word.

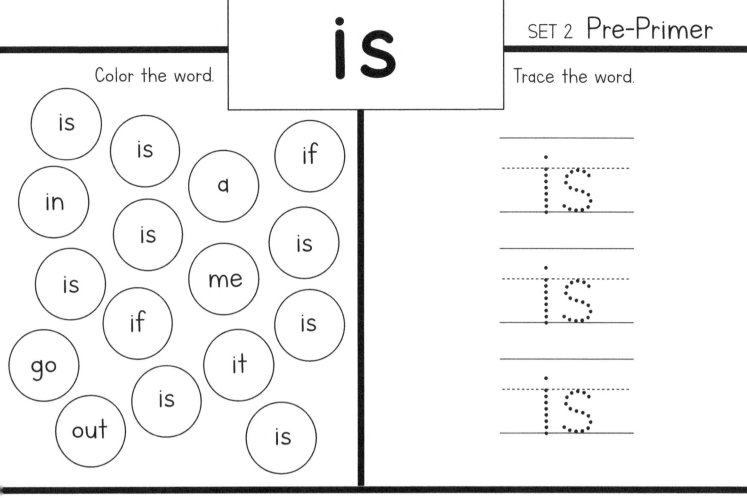

Read the word.

The cap is green.

Write the word.

Spell the word.
< connect the letters >

She _____ nice.

He _____ kind.

it

Color the word.

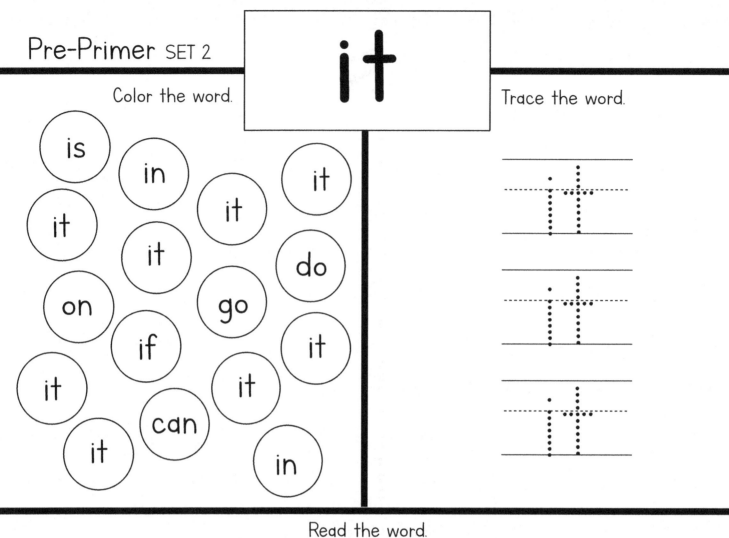

Trace the word.

Read the word.

It went fast.

Write the word.

I like _____.

I see _____.

Spell the word.
< connect the letters >

jump

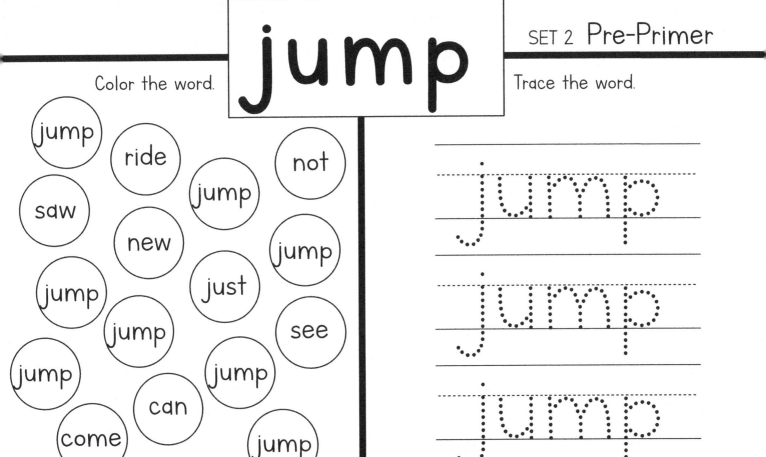

Color the word.

Trace the word.

Read the word.

I can jump.

Write the word.

I can _____.

I will _____.

Let's _____.

Spell the word.
< connect the letters >

little

Color the word.

Trace the word.

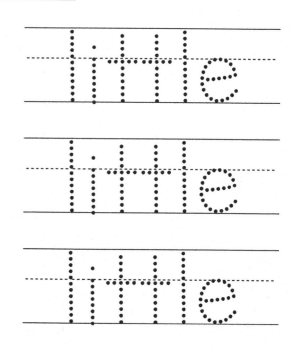

Read the word.

The cat is little.

Write the word.

I found a

_____

rock.

Spell the word.
< connect the letters >

look

Color the word.

Trace the word.

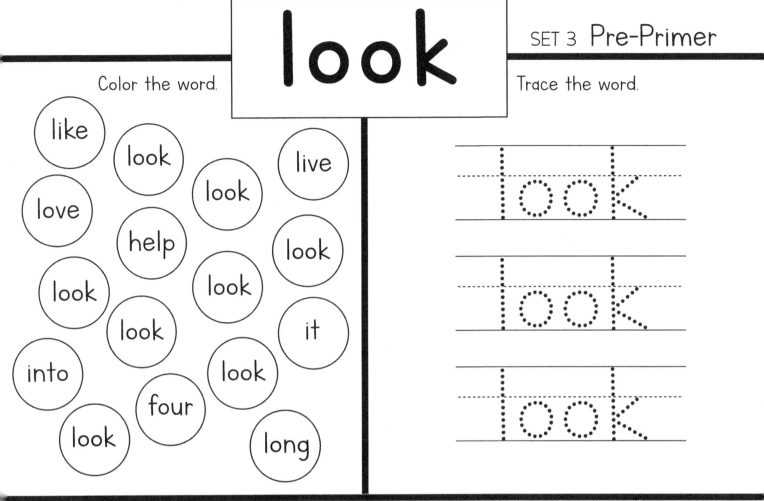

Read the word.

Look at my book.

Write the word.

I _____ at the toys.

Spell the word.
< connect the letters >

make

Color the word.

Trace the word.

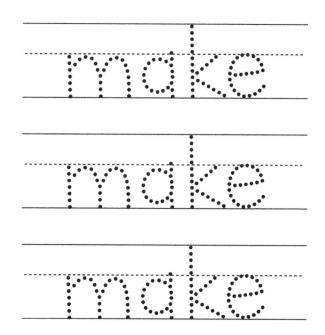

Read the word.

I make my bed.

Write the word.

I can _____

a picture.

Spell the word.
< connect the letters >

me

Color the word.

Trace the word.

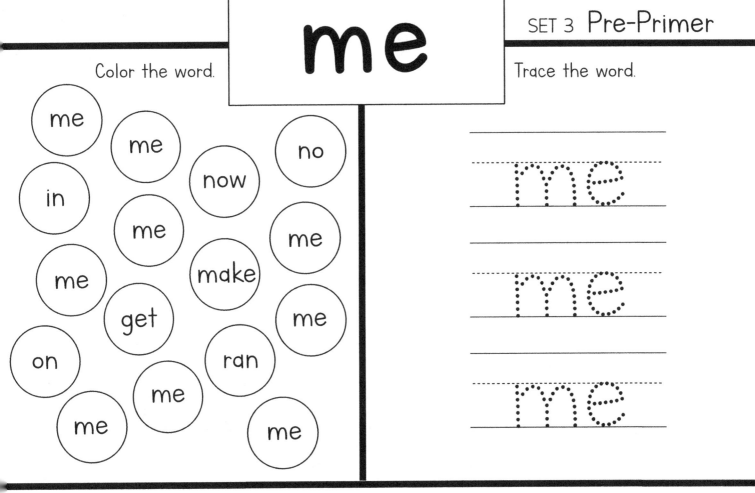

Read the word.

Go with me.

Write the word.

My teacher
helps _____.

Spell the word.
< connect the letters >

my

Color the word.

Trace the word.

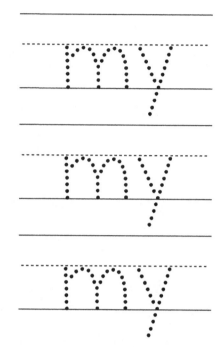

Read the word.

My friend is kind.

Write the word.

I like _____

toy.

Spell the word.
< connect the letters >

not

Color the word.

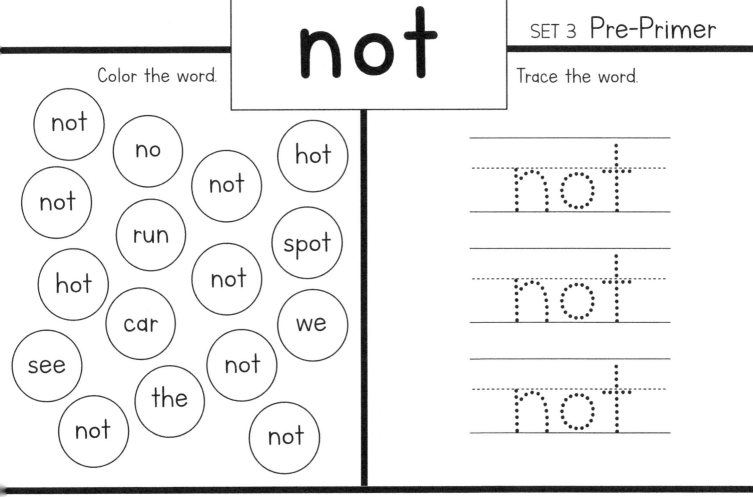

Trace the word.

not
not
not

Read the word.

I do not hit.

Write the word.

There is _____

a cloud in the

sky.

Spell the word.
< connect the letters >

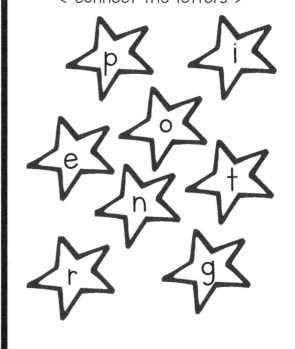

one

Color the word.

Trace the word.

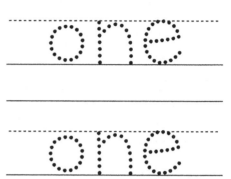

Read the word.

I see one dog.

Write the word.

She has _____

book.

Spell the word.
< connect the letters >

play

Color the word.

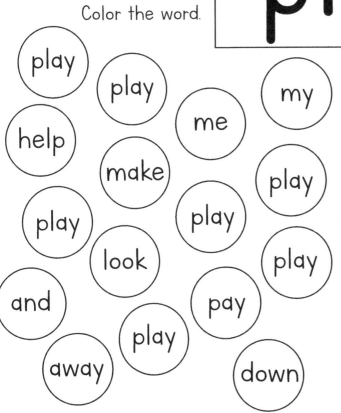

Trace the word.

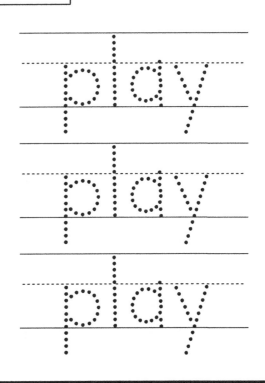

Read the word.

She will play the game.

Write the word.

He can _____ too.

Spell the word.
< connect the letters >

red

Color the word.

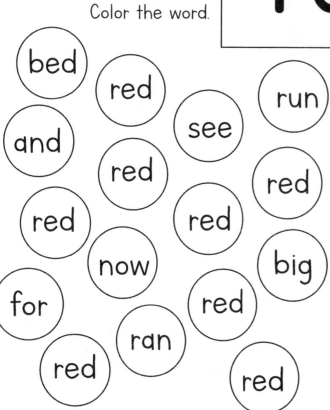

Trace the word.

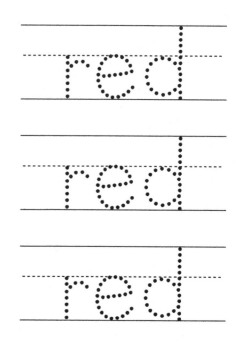

Read the word.

My car is red.

Write the word.

The _____

shirt is big.

Spell the word.
< connect the letters >

run

Color the word.

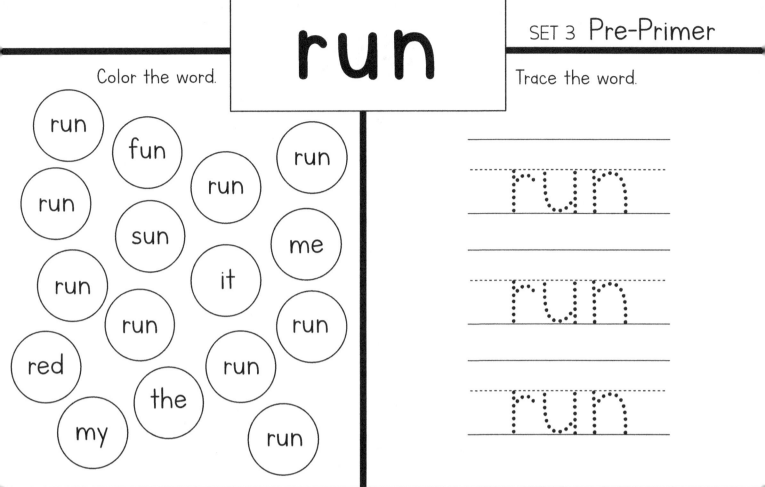

run fun run run
run sun me
run it
run run run
red run
my the run

Trace the word.

run

run

run

Read the word.

I will run.

Write the word.

The girl can ____ fast.

Spell the word.
< connect the letters >

k z c x u r t n

said

Color the word.

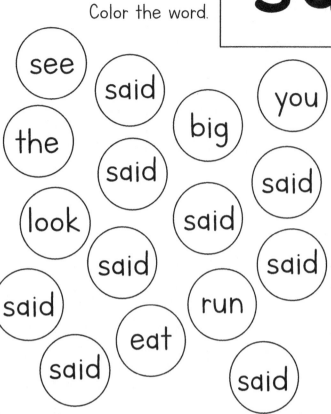

Trace the word.

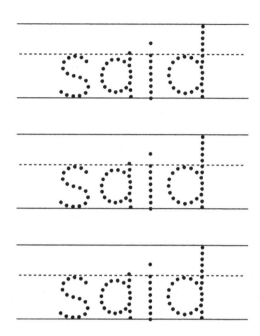

Read the word.

I said it.

Write the word.

She _____,

"It is time to

go."

Spell the word.
< connect the letters >

see

Color the word.

Trace the word.

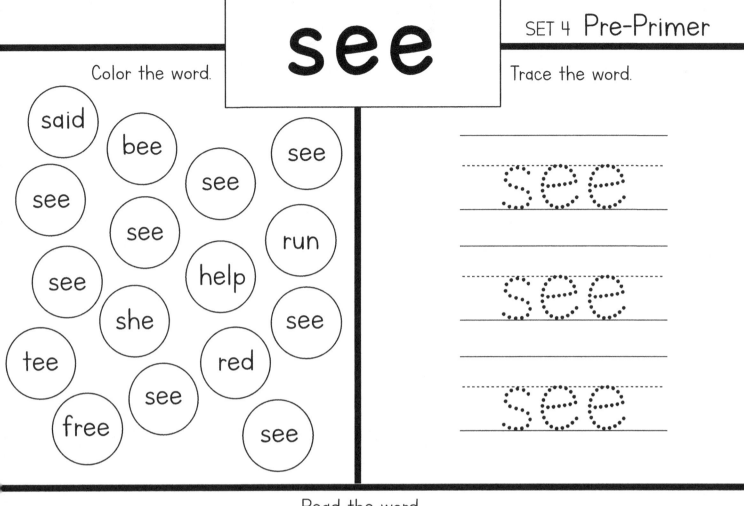

Read the word.

I see the slide.

Write the word.

The cat can

_____ the

toy.

Spell the word.
< connect the letters >

the

Color the word.

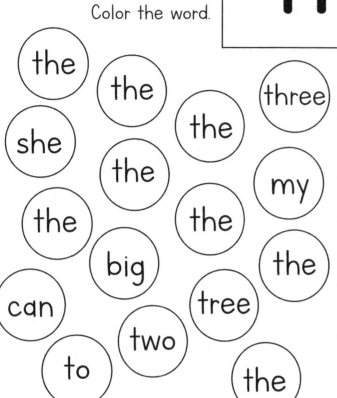

Trace the word.

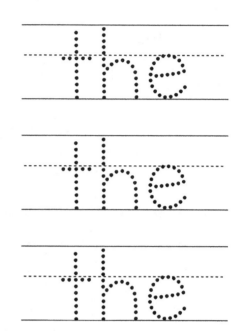

Read the word.

The dog is fun.

Write the word.

I go to

_____

school.

Spell the word.
< connect the letters >

three

Color the word.

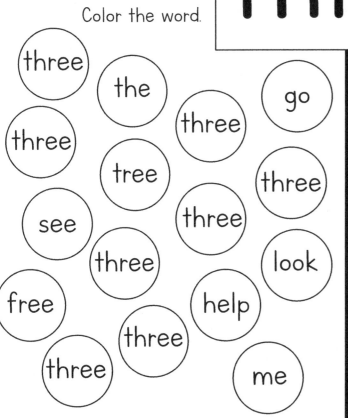

three the three go
three tree three
see three look
free help
three three me

Trace the word.

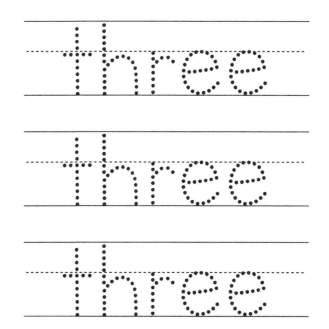

Read the word.

I see three bugs.

Write the word.

The car has

stripes.

Spell the word.
< connect the letters >

to

Color the word.

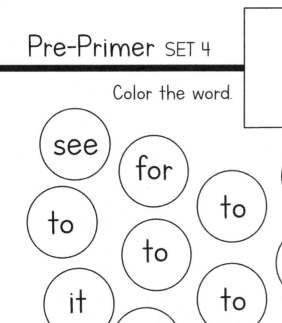

Trace the word.

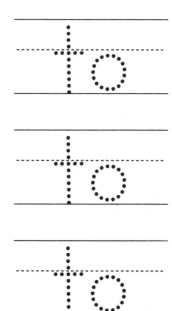

Read the word.

My cat went to her bed.

Write the word.

The bus drove

_____

the

school.

Spell the word.
< connect the letters >

two

Color the word.

Trace the word.

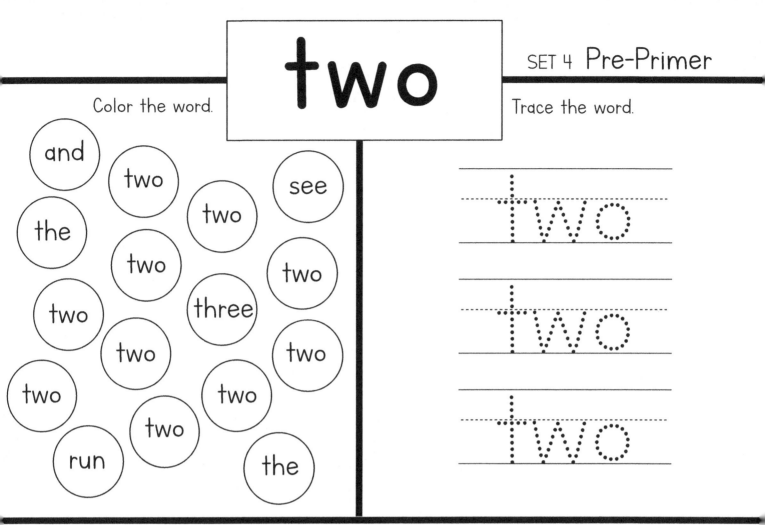

Read the word.

I read two books.

Write the word.

My pet is

years old.

Spell the word.
< connect the letters >

up

Color the word.

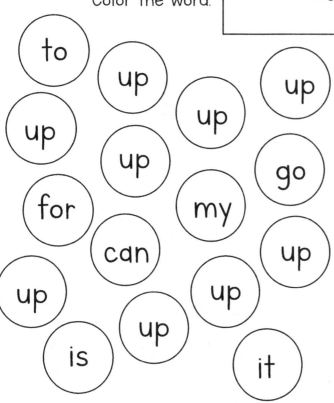

Trace the word.

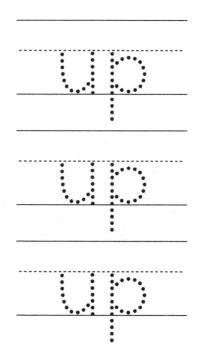

Read the word.

I go up the hill.

Write the word.

Look at the cloud _____ in the sky.

Spell the word.
< connect the letters >

we

Color the word.

Trace the word.

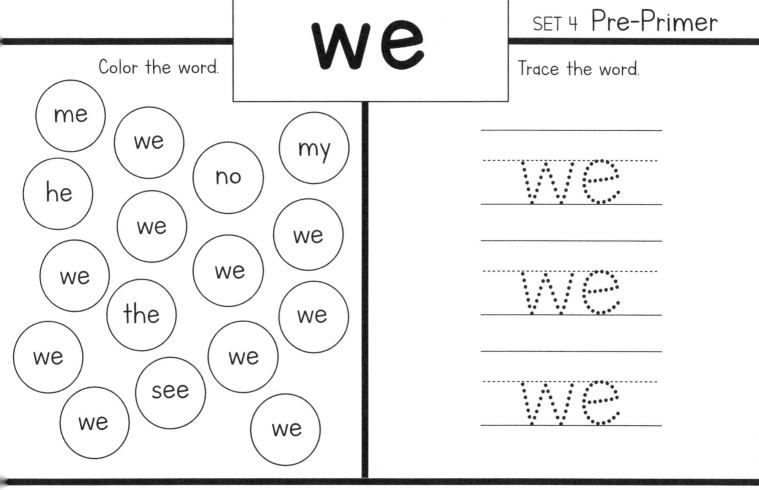

Read the word.

We go to the park.

Write the word.

Will
be home
soon?

Spell the word.
< connect the letters >

where

Color the word.

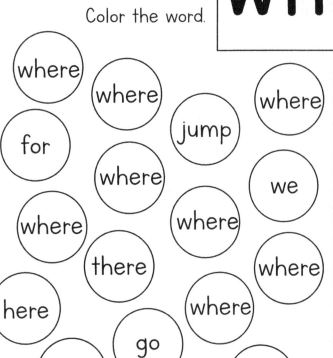

Trace the word.

Read the word.

Where did the toy go?

Write the word.

I did not see

_____

_____ my

kitten went.

Spell the word.
< connect the letters >

yellow

Color the word.

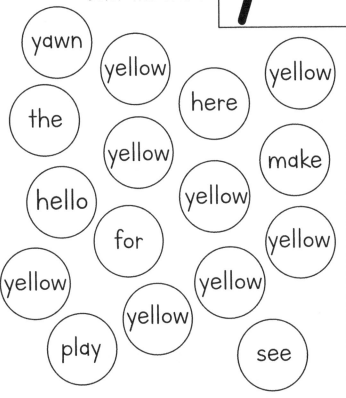

Trace the word.

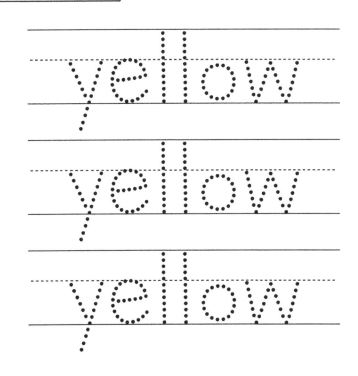

Read the word.

I see a yellow block.

Write the word.

I will stack the _____ block.

Spell the word.
< connect the letters >

you

Color the word.

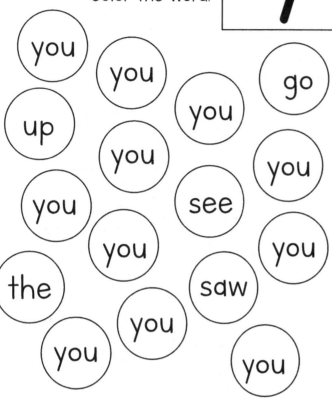

you · you · you · go · up · you · you · you · you · see · you · you · the · saw · you · you · you

Trace the word.

you
you
you

Read the word.

You see the red cap.

Write the word.

I see _____

work hard and

do your best.

Spell the word.
< connect the letters >

EXTRA
Activities
Pre-Primer

```
c  d  o  w  n  b  i  g
o  q  r  j (a  n  d) b
m  p  t  a  w  a  y  n
e  b  l  u  e  f  o  r
f  i  n  d  a  v  k  t
c  a  n  t  n  l  m  g
```

~~and~~   blue   down

away   can   find

big   come   for

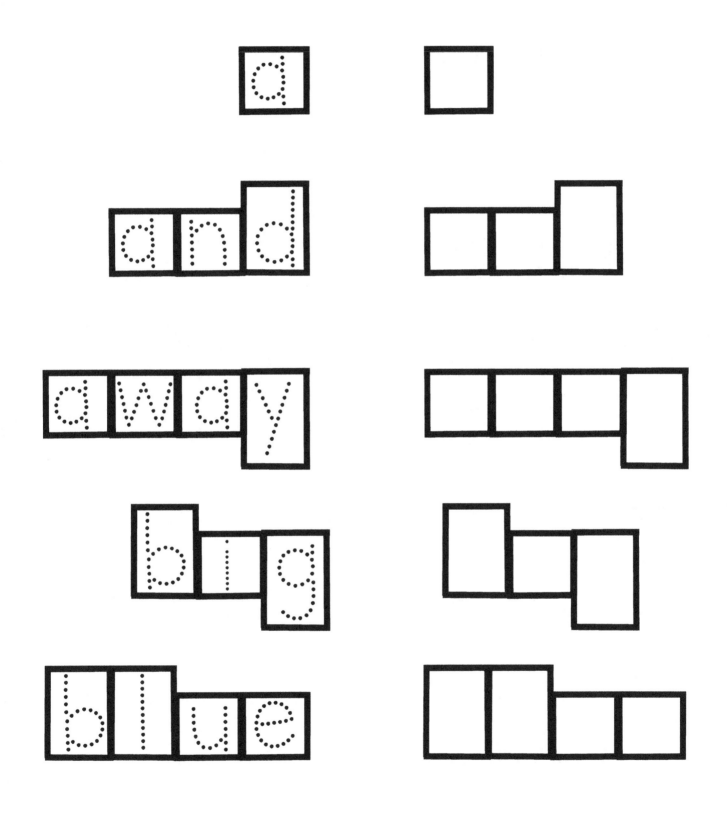

Pre-Primer SET 1

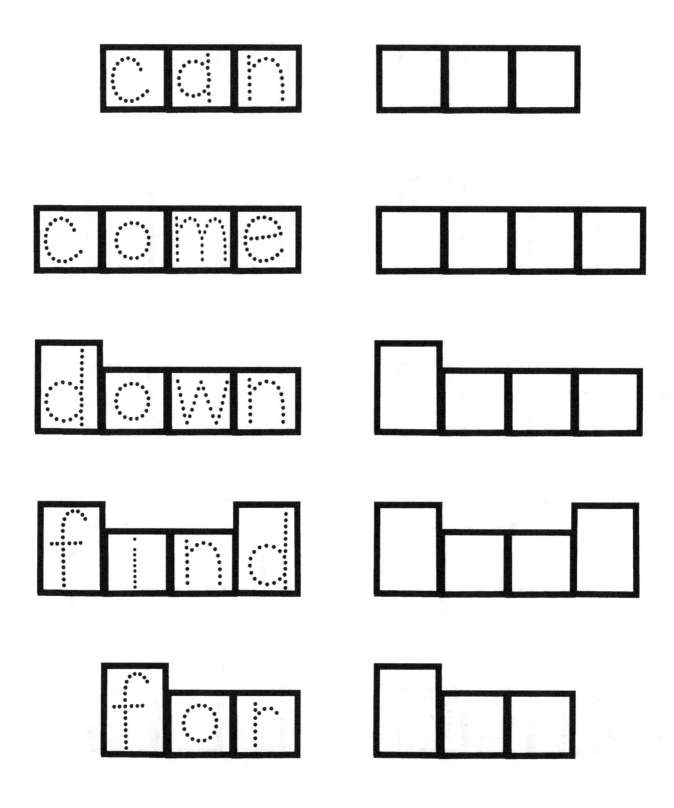

a   away   blue   come   find

and   big   can   ~~down~~   for

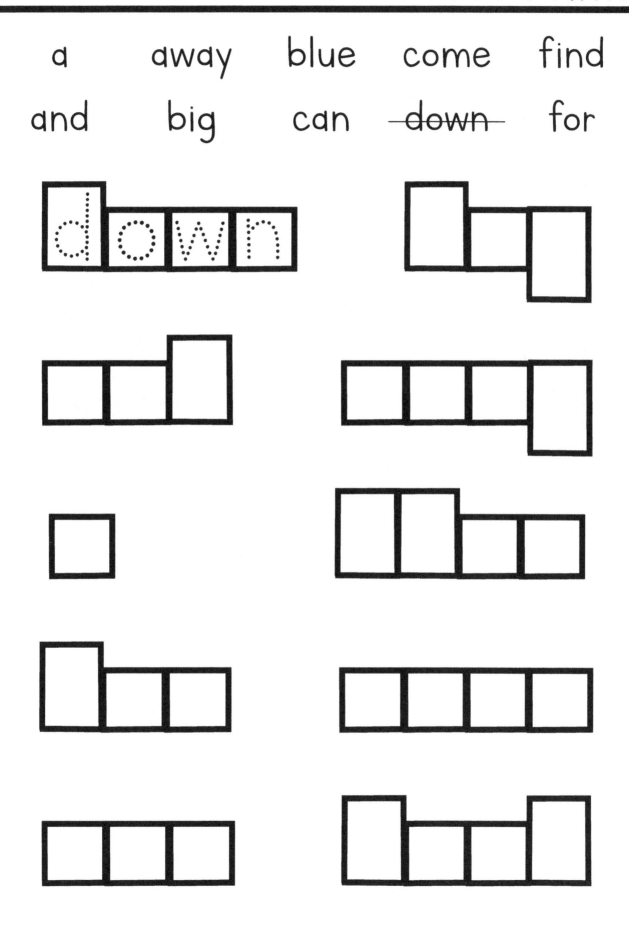

f	h	j	u	m	p	q	q
u	e	i	s	i	n	r	p
n	l	l	i	t	t	l	e
n	p	h	e	r	e	m	p
y	g	o	i	t	I	x	b

funny	here	it
go	I	jump
help	in	little
	is	

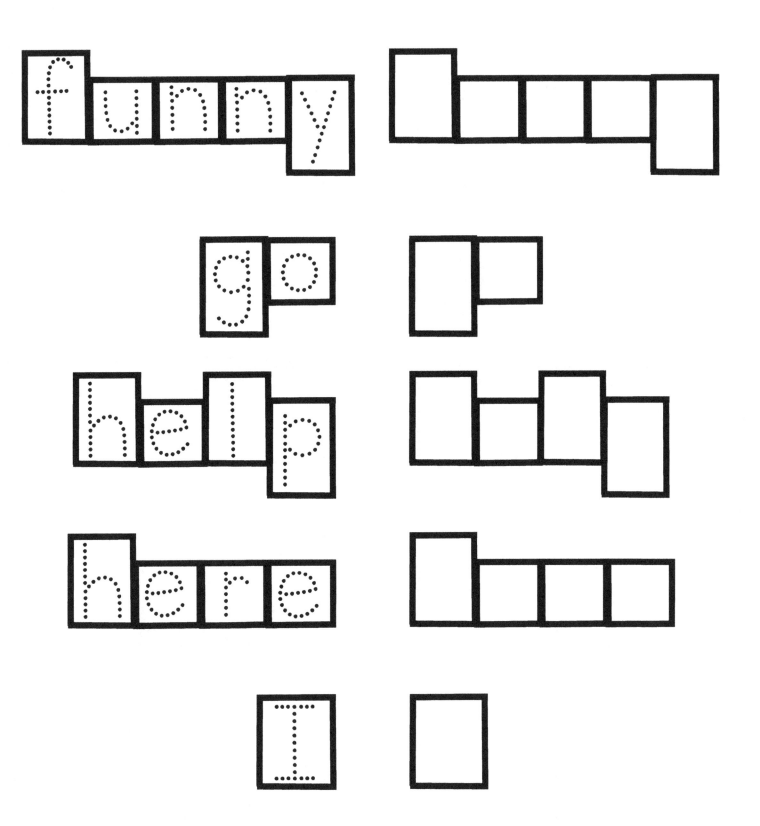

Pre-Primer SET 2

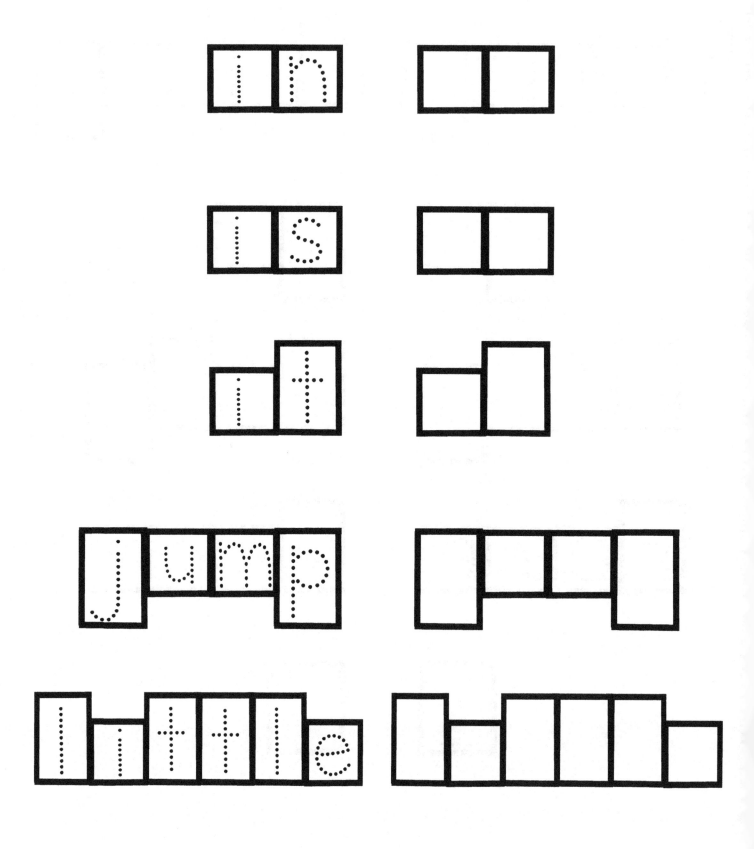

funny   help   I   is   jump

go   here   ~~in~~   it   little

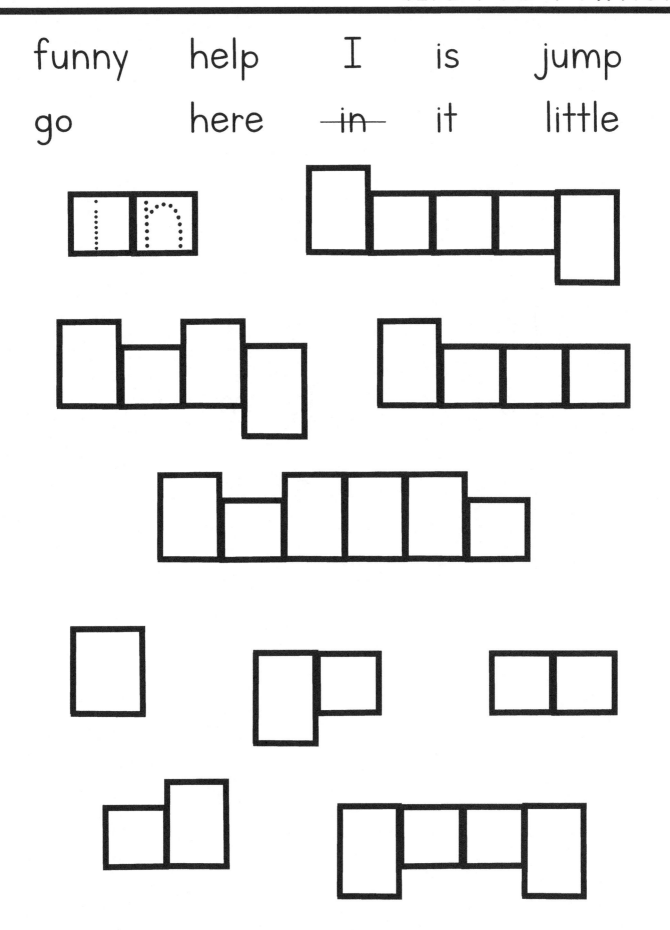

```
y   a   l   p   o   n

m   y   z   n   u   m

k   d   e   r   a   t

o   n   i   k   m   d

o   o   e   a   e   e

l   t   p   r   s   y
```

~~look~~   me   not   play   run

make   my   one   red   said

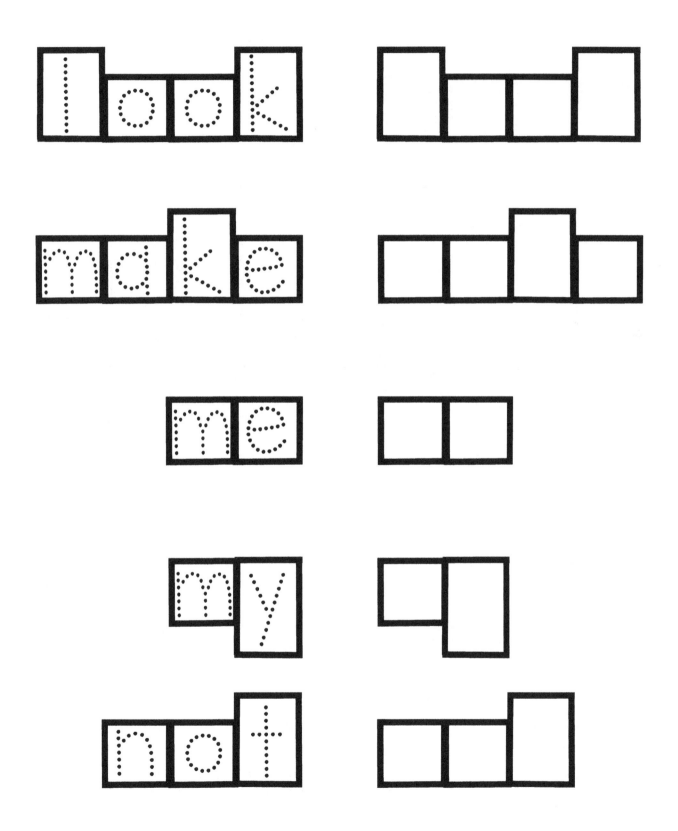

Pre-Primer SET 3

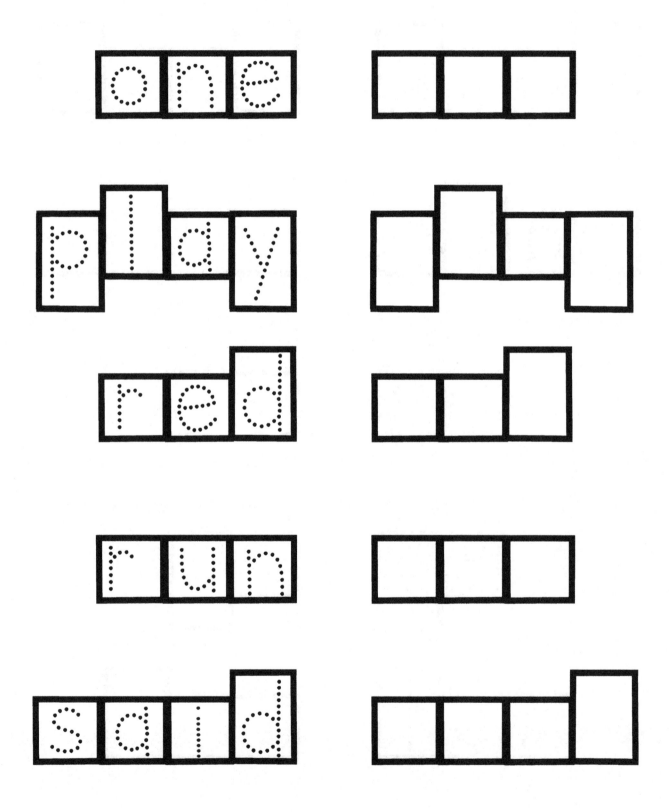

look me not play run

make my one red ~~said~~

said

```
v   m   w   u   t   y
s   e   o   h   e   e
e   y   r   l   r   q
e   e   l   e   h   t
e   o   h   u   w   b
w   w   t   o   p   y
```

~~see~~   to   where

the   two   yellow

three   up   you

we

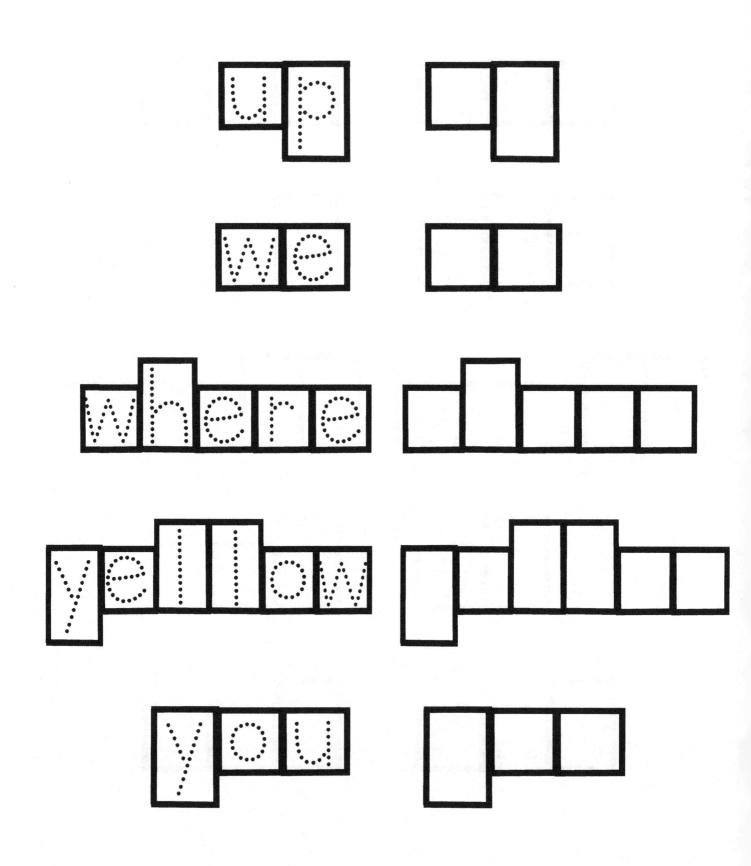

see   three   two   we   ~~yellow~~

the   to   up   where   you

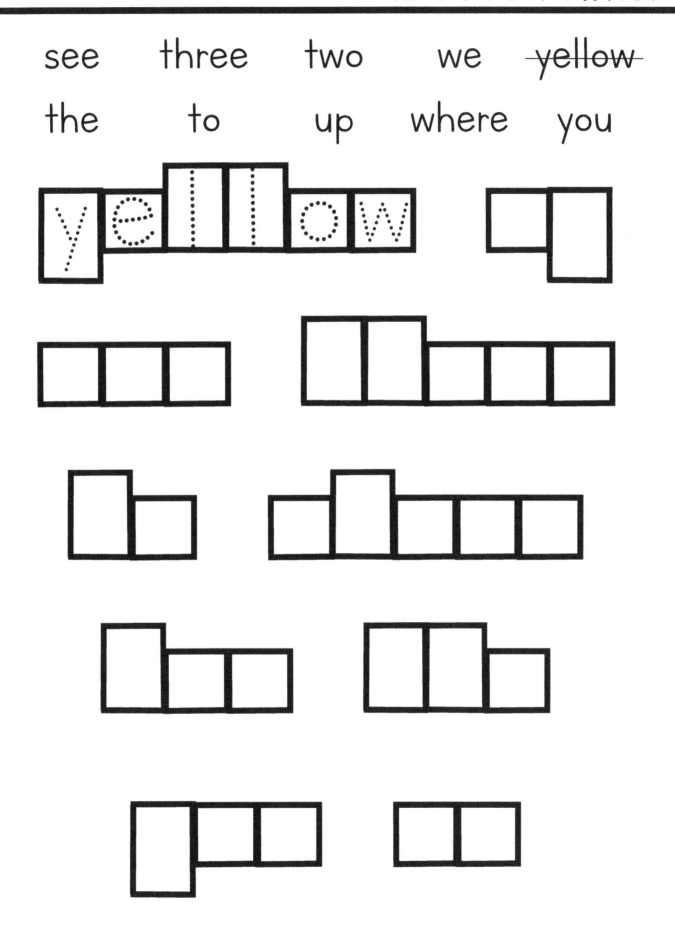

Primer

all

Color the word.

Trace the word.

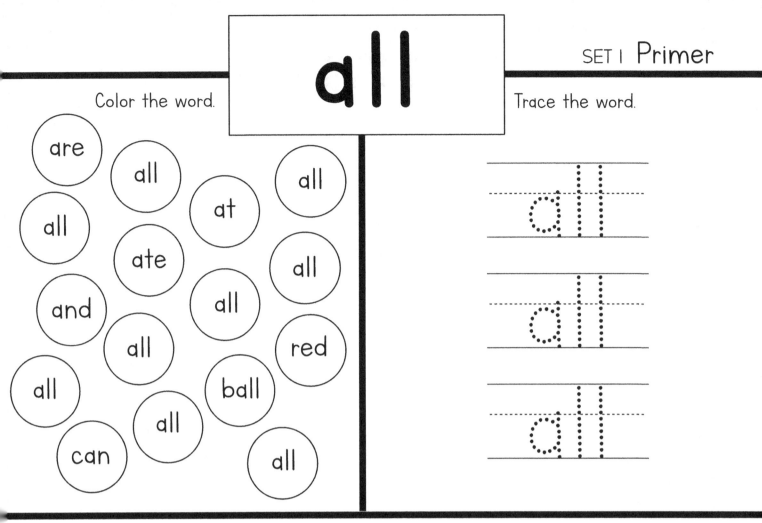

are · all · all · all · at · all · all · ate · all · and · all · red · all · ball · can · all · all

Read the word.

I see all the cows.

Write the word.

I pick up of my toys.

Spell the word.
< connect the letters >

a · e · l · y · l · u · r · f

am

Color the word.

are · all · am · am · am · am · am · ham · at · am · ate · arm · am · am · mat

Trace the word.

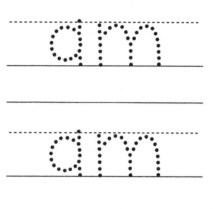

am
am
am

Read the word.

I am kind.

Write the word.

I ____ going to the park.

Spell the word.
< connect the letters >

g · c · w · t · d · m · p · f

are

Color the word.

are

are

ate

bare

are

are

are

all

are

care

ran

far

are

are

am

are

Trace the word.

are

are

are

Read the word.

Are you funny?

Write the word.

How far away

_____ you?

Spell the word.
< connect the letters >

at

Color the word.

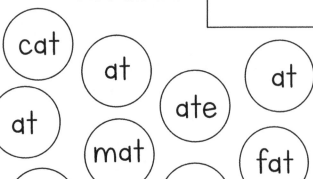
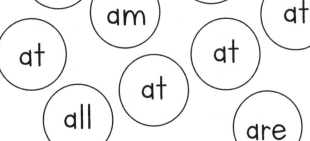

cat, at, at, at, ate, mat, fat, at, at, am, at, at, at, at, all, are

Trace the word.

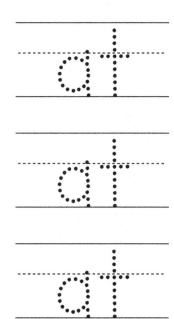

Read the word.

She is at the store.

Write the word.

Throw the ball _____ your coach.

Spell the word.
< connect the letters >

e i r n p d m t

ate

Color the word.

Trace the word.

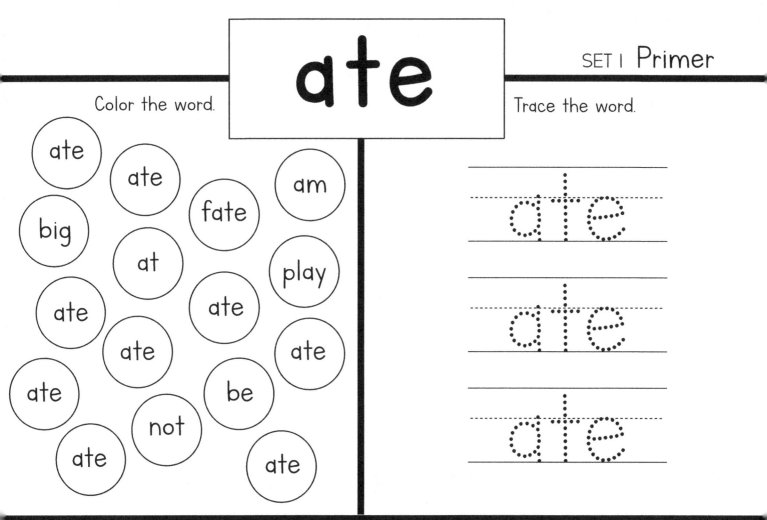

Read the word.

She ate her lunch.

Write the word.

The dog _____

his bone.

Spell the word.
< connect the letters >

be

Color the word.

Trace the word.

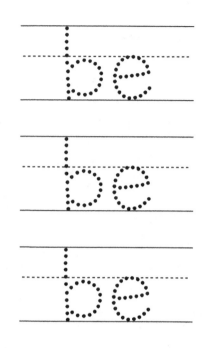

Read the word.

I will be nice.

Write the word.

The cat will ___ fun to play with.

Spell the word.
< connect the letters >

black

Color the word.

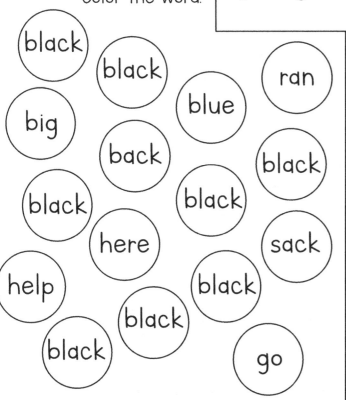

Trace the word.

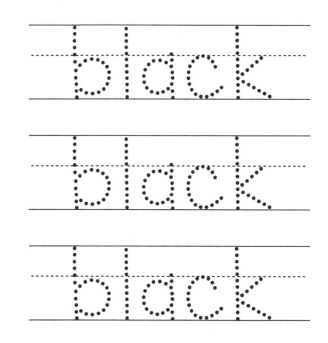

Read the word.

The cat is black.

Write the word.

My _____

pen is lost.

Spell the word.
< connect the letters >

brown

Color the word.

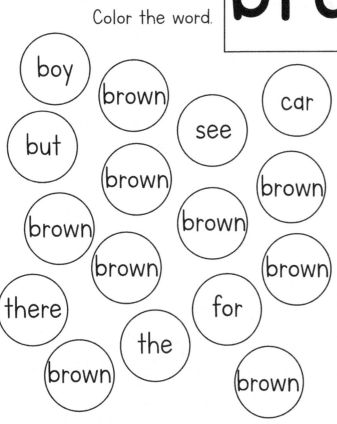

boy | brown | car | see | but | brown | brown | brown | brown | brown | brown | there | brown | for | the | brown

Trace the word.

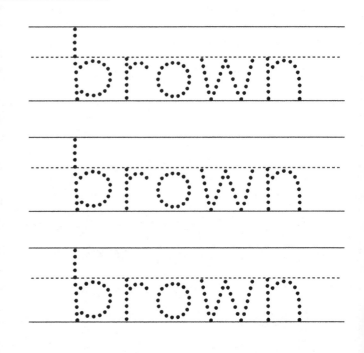

Read the word.

The cat is brown.

Write the word.

I see the

_____

tree.

Spell the word.
< connect the letters >

e   b   r   o   w   d   b   n

but

Color the word.

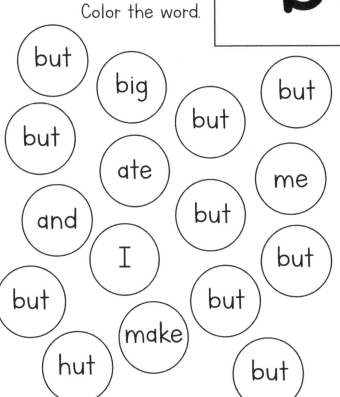

Trace the word.

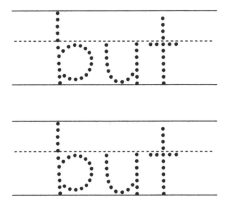

Read the word.

I am small but strong.

Write the word.

The book is

big _____

good.

Spell the word.
< connect the letters >

came

Color the word.

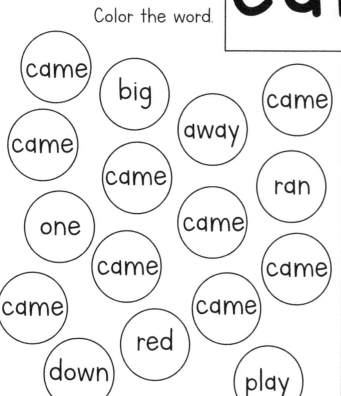

Trace the word.

Read the word.

My mom came home.

Write the word.

She _____

with us on

the bus.

Spell the word.
< connect the letters >

did

Color the word.

did

did

hid

can

dad

did

did

did

did

did

me

did

my

mom

did

did

did

Trace the word.

did

did

did

Read the word.

I did go.

Write the word.

The dog

dig a hole.

Spell the word.
< connect the letters >

do

Color the word.

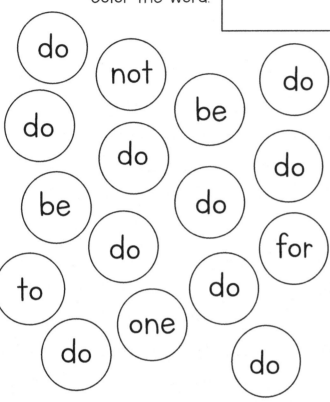

Trace the word.

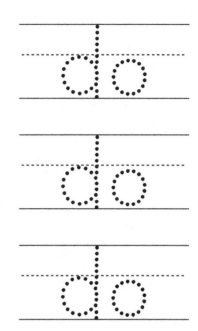

Read the word.

I will do the job.

Write the word.

Do not _____ that.

Spell the word.
< connect the letters >

eat

Color the word.

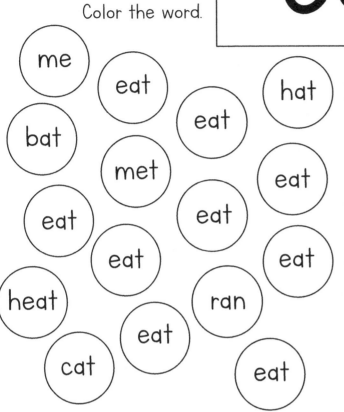

me

eat

hat

bat

eat

met

eat

eat

eat

eat

eat

heat

ran

eat

cat

eat

Trace the word.

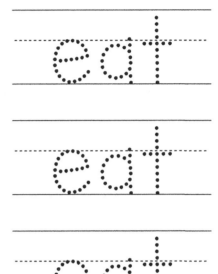

eat

eat

eat

Read the word.

The dog will eat.

Write the word.

She will

the food.

Spell the word.
< connect the letters >

four

Color the word.

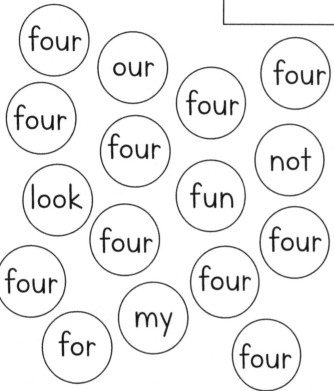

Trace the word.

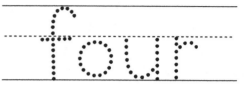
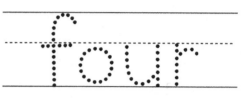
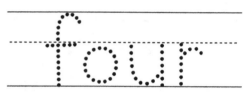

Read the word.

She is four.

Write the word.

The cat has

_____ toys.

Spell the word.
< connect the letters >

get

Color the word.

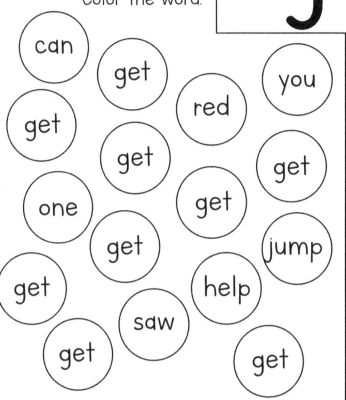

can
get
get
get
one
get
get
saw
get

you
red
get
get
jump
help
get

Trace the word.

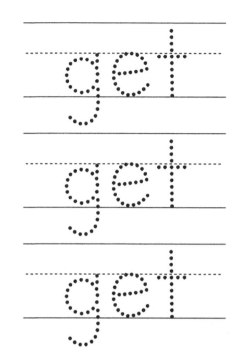

Read the word.

I will get a hat.

Write the word.

He will _____

his book.

Spell the word.
< connect the letters >

good

Color the word.

Trace the word.

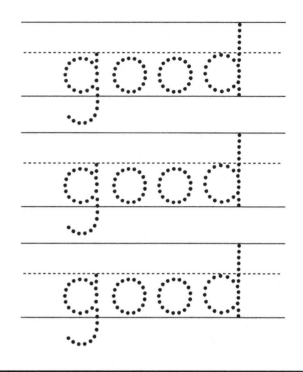

Read the word.

I am good at ball.

Write the word.

She is a

_____ dog.

Spell the word.
< connect the letters >

have

Color the word.

Trace the word.

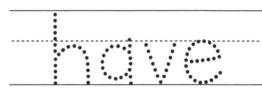

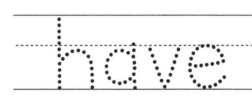

Read the word.

I have a toy.

Write the word.

You _____

a ball.

Spell the word.
< connect the letters >

he

Color the word.

Trace the word.

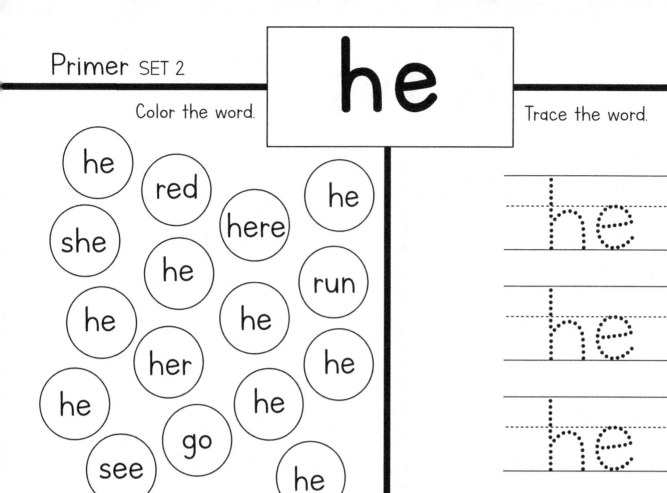

Read the word.

He is a kid.

Write the word.

Is _____ tall?

Spell the word.
< connect the letters >

into

Color the word.

Trace the word.

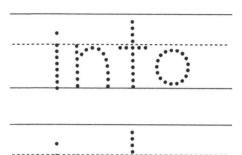

Read the word.

I went into the park.

Write the word.

The cat ran

the box.

Spell the word.
< connect the letters >

like

Color the word.

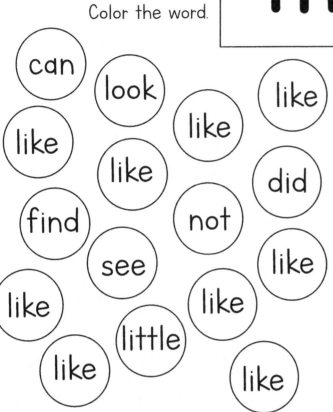

can look like
like like did
like find not like
see
like little like like
like like

Trace the word.

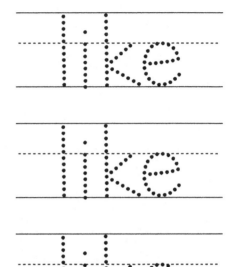

Read the word.

I like to go.

Write the word.

I do not

_____
....
_____ it.

Spell the word.
< connect the letters >

must

Color the word.

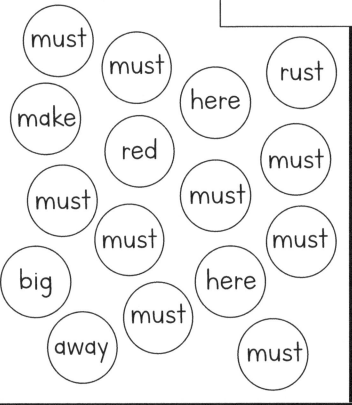

Trace the word.

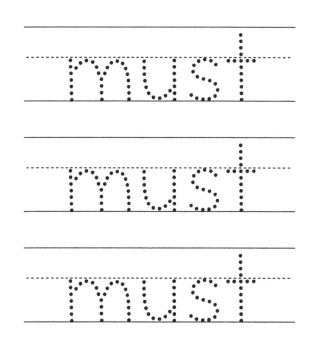

Read the word.

I must go to bed.

Write the word.

The dog

_____ get

the ball.

Spell the word.
< connect the letters >

new

Color the word.

Trace the word.

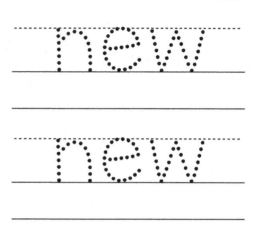

Read the word.

The book is new.

Write the word.

I see my
_____ toy.

Spell the word.
< connect the letters >

no

Color the word.

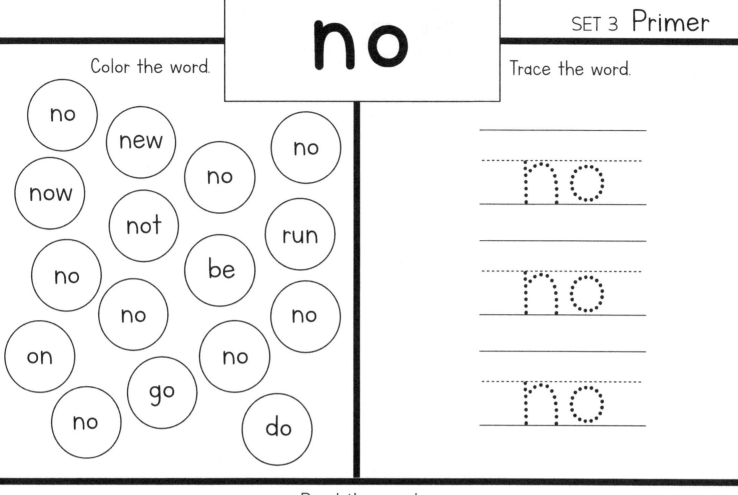

Trace the word.

no

no

no

Read the word.

I see no toys.

Write the word.

He has _____

paper to

draw on.

Spell the word.
< connect the letters >

now

Color the word.

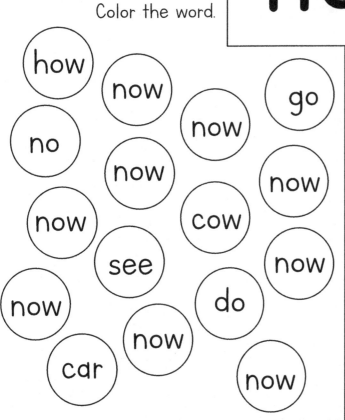

Trace the word.

Read the word.

I will go to the bus now.

Write the word.

The car will

go _____

from school.

Spell the word.
< connect the letters >

on

Color the word.

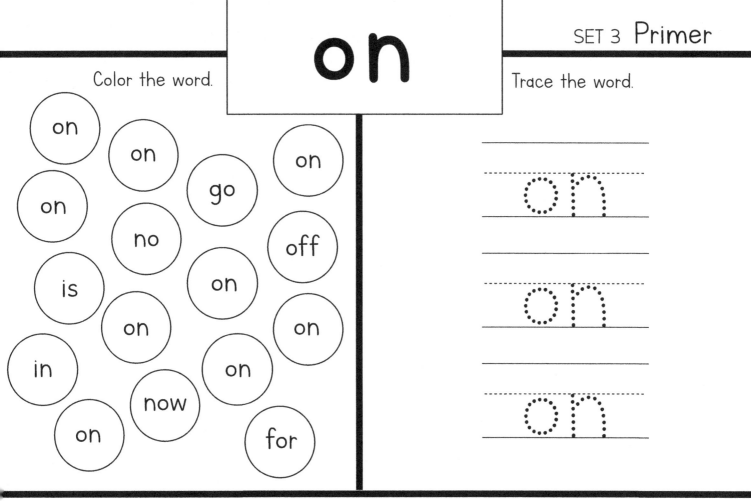

Trace the word.

Read the word.

The book is on top.

Write the word.

I put my toy
___ my bed.

Spell the word.
< connect the letters >

our

Color the word.

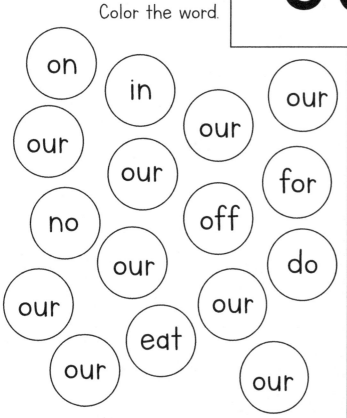

Trace the word.

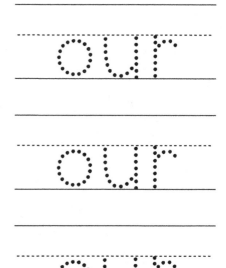

Read the word.

This is our home.

Write the word.

We ride

_____ bus.

Spell the word.
< connect the letters >

out

Color the word.

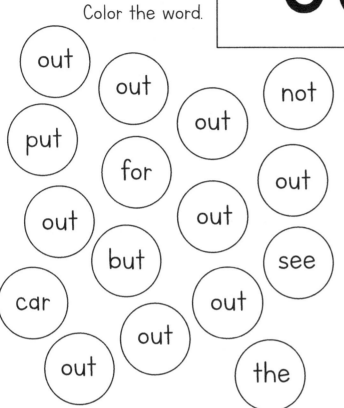

Trace the word.

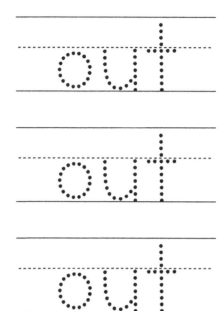

Read the word.

The dog went out.

Write the word.

I go _____

the door.

Spell the word.
< connect the letters >

please

Color the word.

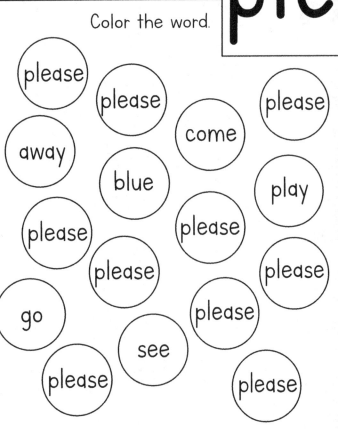

Trace the word.

Read the word.

I say please.

Write the word.

Hand me
my ball,

_____
_ _ _ _ _ _ _ _ _
_____ .

Spell the word.
< connect the letters >

pretty

Color the word.

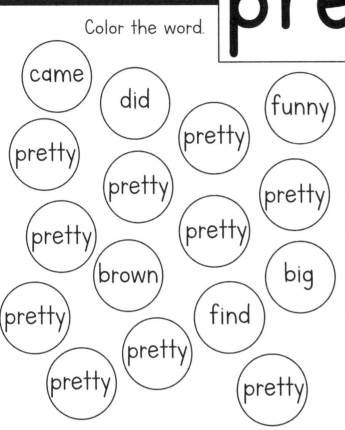

came did funny
pretty pretty
pretty pretty
pretty pretty
pretty brown big
pretty find
pretty
pretty pretty

Trace the word.

pretty

pretty

pretty

Read the word.

I saw a pretty dog.

Write the word.

I made a

_____

picture.

Spell the word.
< connect the letters >

e t
t
r
p y
b s

ran

Color the word.

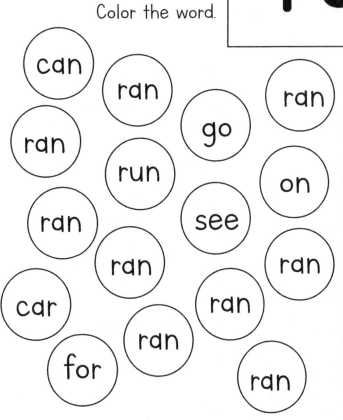

Trace the word.

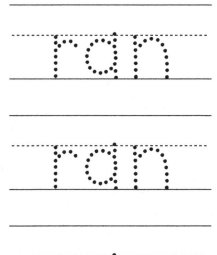

Read the word.

The boy ran.

Write the word.

A bug

_____
_____

Spell the word.
< connect the letters >

ride

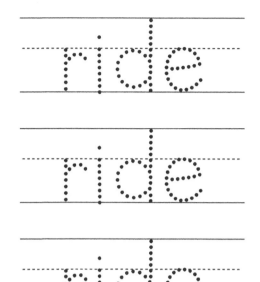

Color the word.

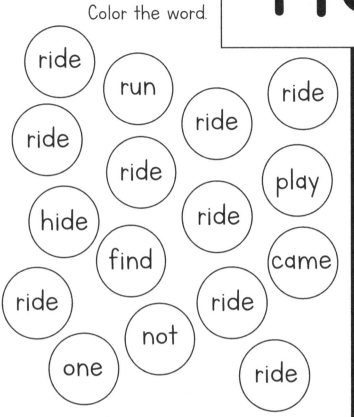

Trace the word.

ride
ride
ride

Read the word.

I ride a bike.

Write the word.

She will go for a

_____
_____ .

Spell the word.
< connect the letters >

saw

Color the word.

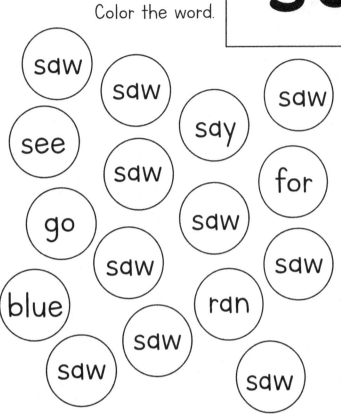

saw · saw · saw · say · see · saw · for · go · saw · saw · saw · blue · ran · saw · saw

Trace the word.

Read the word.

He saw a red car.

Write the word.

The cow _____ the food.

Spell the word.
< connect the letters >

say

Color the word.

Trace the word.

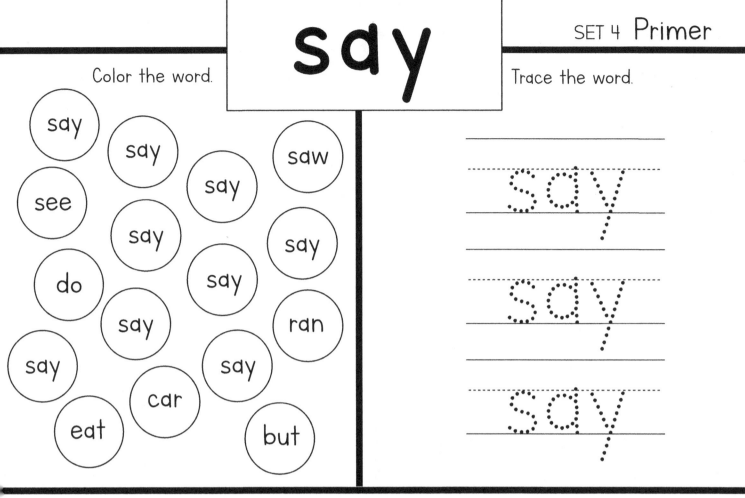

say say saw
see say
say say
do say
say say ran
say say
car
eat but

say
say
say

Read the word.

I say hi.

Write the word.

She will

_____ it.

Spell the word.
< connect the letters >

s j
d
u
b
y
t e

she

Color the word.

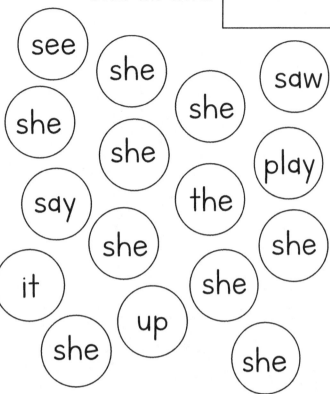

Trace the word.

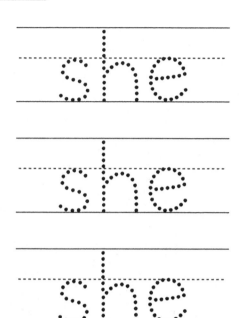

Read the word.

She helps.

Write the word.

Where does

_____

_____ play?

Spell the word.
< connect the letters >

SO

Color the word.

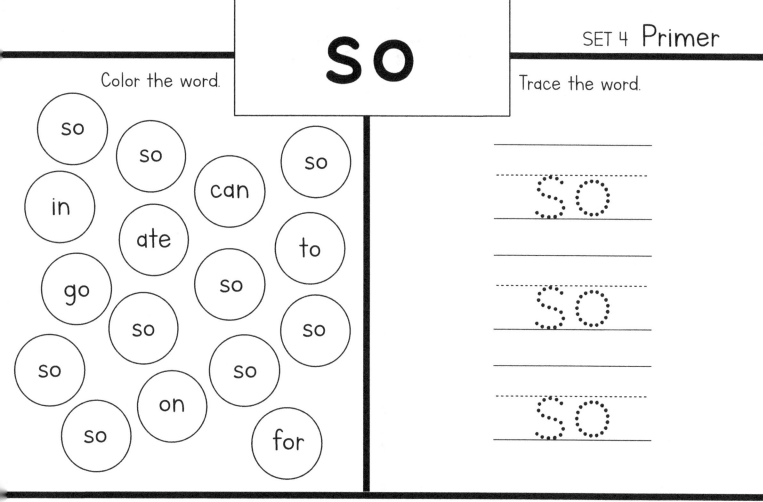

Trace the word.

SO

SO

SO

Read the word.

The car is so fast.

Write the word.

I am _____

happy.

Spell the word.
< connect the letters >

soon

Color the word.

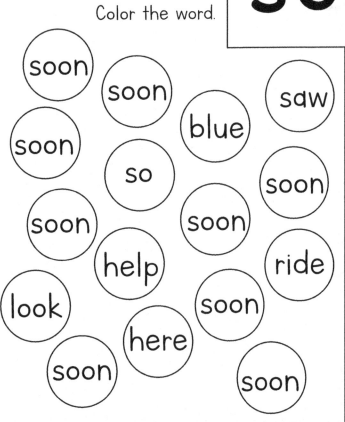

Trace the word.

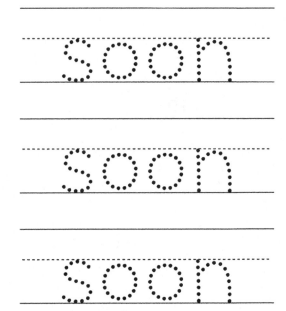

Read the word.

He will go soon.

Write the word.

I will eat

_____

_____

_____ .

Spell the word.
< connect the letters >

that

Color the word.

Trace the word.

that   the   for   that
this   that   car
that   two   not   that
      came   that
that   that
three   that

that
that
that

Read the word.

I see that ball.

Write the word.

I read _____ book.

Spell the word.
< connect the letters >

there

Color the word.

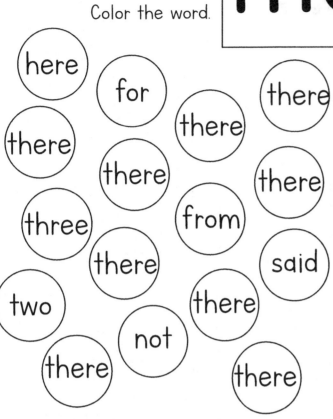

Trace the word.

Read the word.

The man will go there.

Write the word.

It is _____

by the box.

Spell the word.
< connect the letters >

they

Color the word.

they three they the they they to see they said they red they they

Trace the word.

they
they
they

Read the word.

They went home.

Write the word.

What did

_____

_____

say?

Spell the word.
< connect the letters >

m o t y h q e b

this

Color the word.

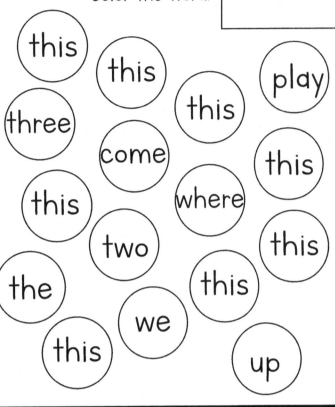

Trace the word.

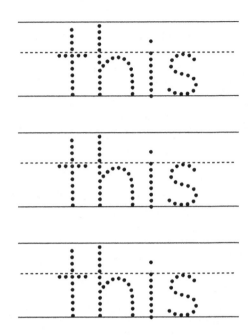

Read the word.

I pet this dog.

Write the word.

I see

one.

Spell the word.
< connect the letters >

too

Color the word.

Trace the word.

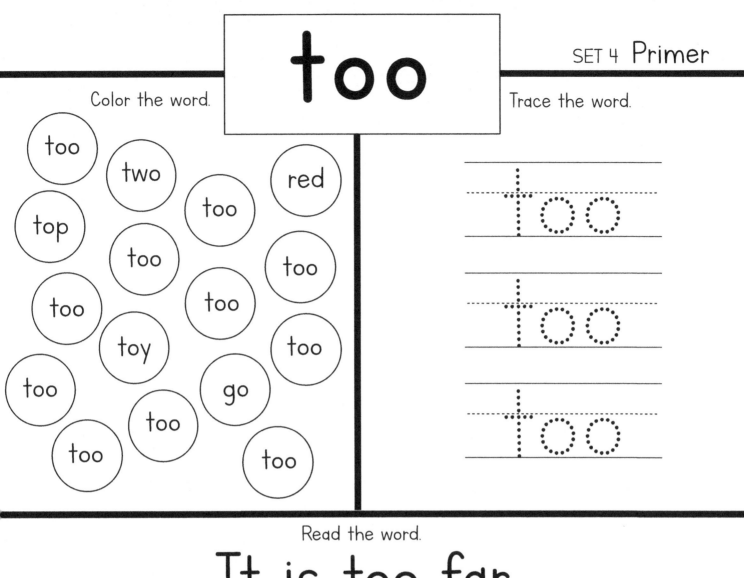

too two red top too too too too too toy too too too go too too

Read the word.

It is too far.

Write the word.

I am

_____

.

Spell the word.
< connect the letters >

under

Color the word.

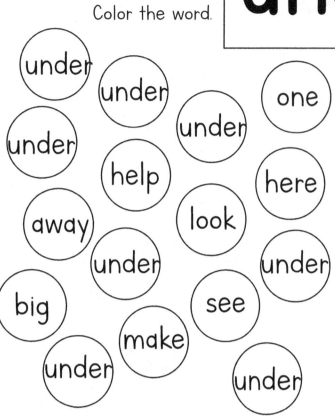

Trace the word.

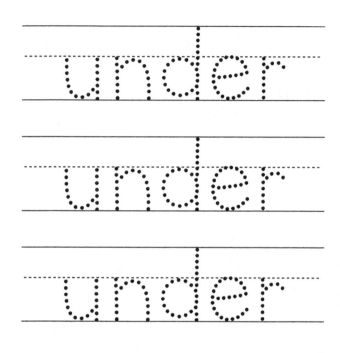

Read the word.

He is under it.

Write the word.

The car drove

_____

- - - - - - - - - - - - - - - - - - -

_____ .

Spell the word.
< connect the letters >

want

Color the word.

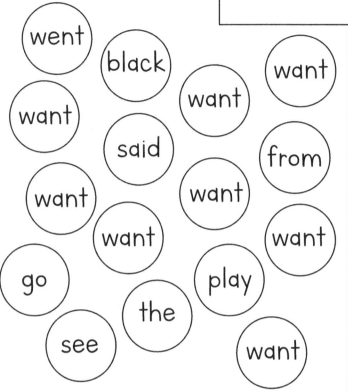

went, black, want, want, want, said, want, want, want, from, want, go, play, want, the, see, want

Trace the word.

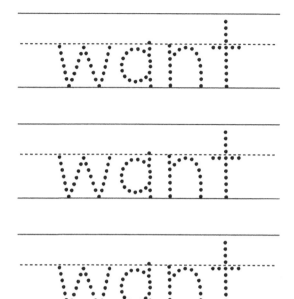

Read the word.

I want the ball.

Write the word.

I do not

_____

to go.

Spell the word.
< connect the letters >

was

Color the word.

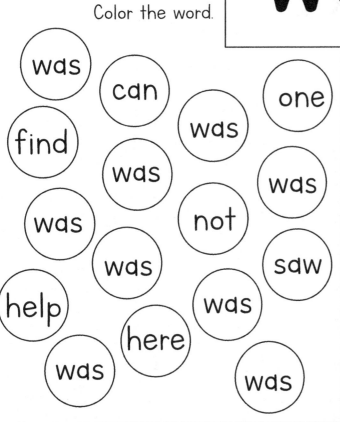

Trace the word.

was
was
was

Read the word.

He was kind.

Write the word.

She _____

fast.

Spell the word.
< connect the letters >

well

Color the word.

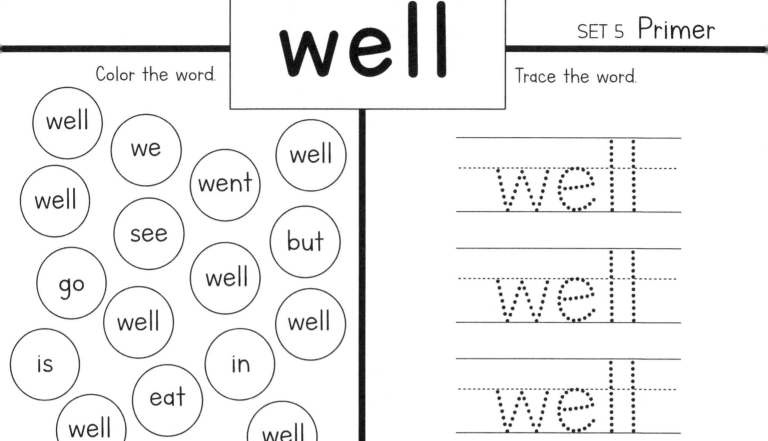

Trace the word.

well
well
well

Read the word.

I am well.

Write the word.

He draws

_____
. . . .
_____ .

Spell the word.
< connect the letters >

went

Color the word.

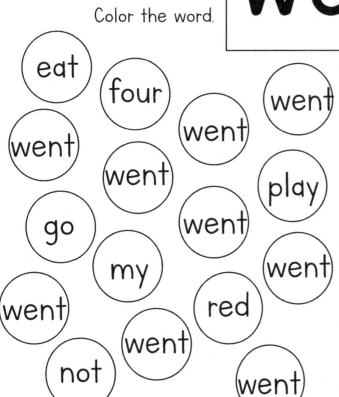

Trace the word.

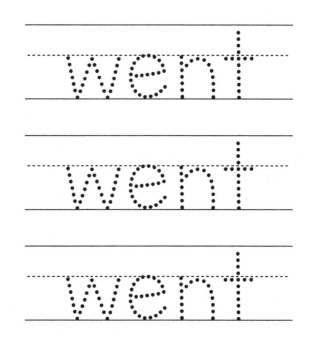

Read the word.

He went.

Write the word.

The cat

home.

Spell the word.
< connect the letters >

what

Color the word.

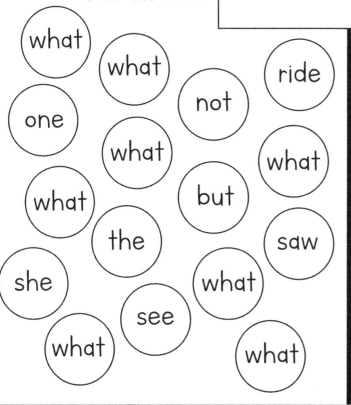

Trace the word.

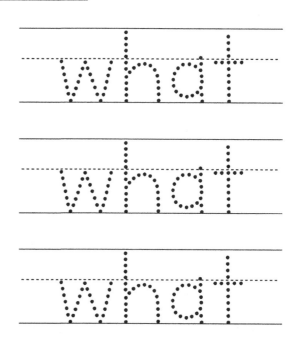

Read the word.

What is it?

Write the word.

I do not know

_____ it is.

Spell the word.
< connect the letters >

white

Color the word.

Trace the word.

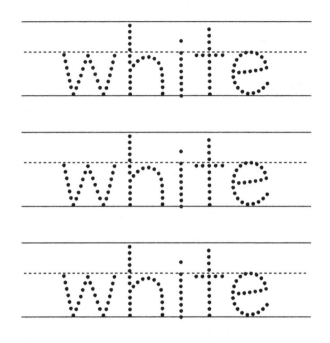

Read the word.

It is white.

Write the word.

The car is

_____

- - - - - - - - - - - - -

_____ .

Spell the word.
< connect the letters >

who

Color the word.

Trace the word.

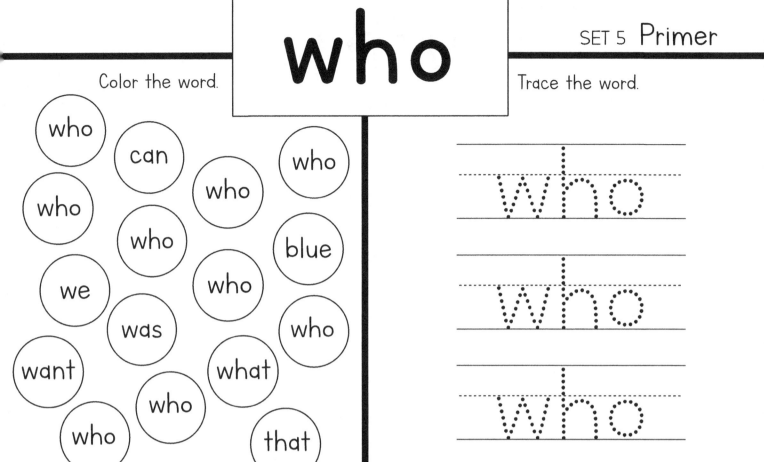

Read the word.

Who is it?

Write the word.

I see ___

that is.

Spell the word.
< connect the letters >

will

Color the word.

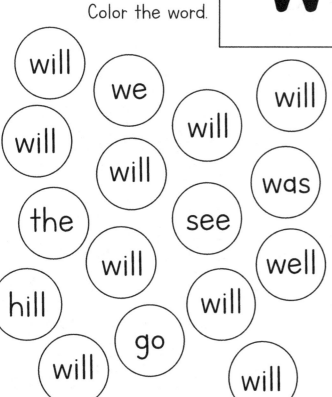

Trace the word.

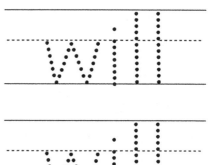

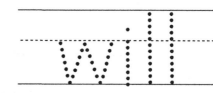

Read the word.

I will go.

Write the word.

She _____

sing.

Spell the word.
< connect the letters >

with

Color the word.

with · with · with · see

what · we · with

with · went · with

the · what · you · with · with

Trace the word.

with

with

with

Read the word.

He is with me.

Write the word.

The dog will

go

the cat.

Spell the word.
< connect the letters >

h · e · t · f · r · i · z · w

yes

Color the word.

Trace the word.

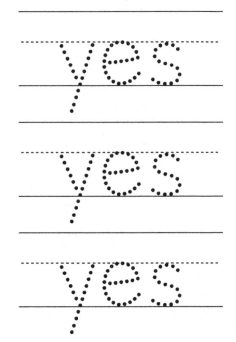

Read the word.

Yes, he will.

Write the word.

Did mom say

_____ ?

Spell the word.
< connect the letters >

EXTRA
Activities
Primer

b a t (a l l) n

l a r e a t e

a m b r o w n

c a m e b u t

k d i d b e t

all	ate	brown
am	be	but
are	black	came
at		did

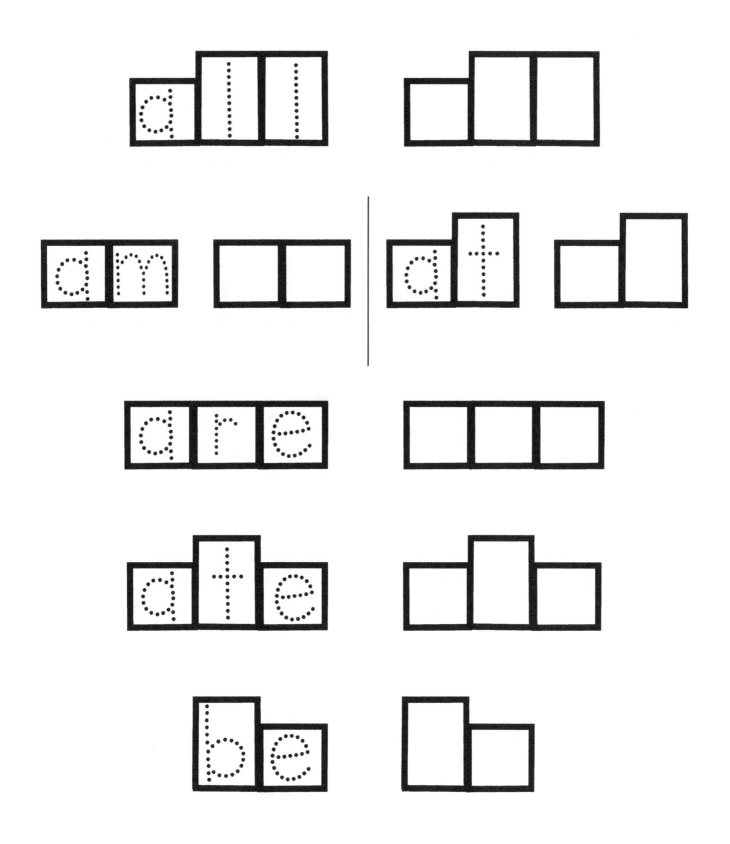

Primer SET I

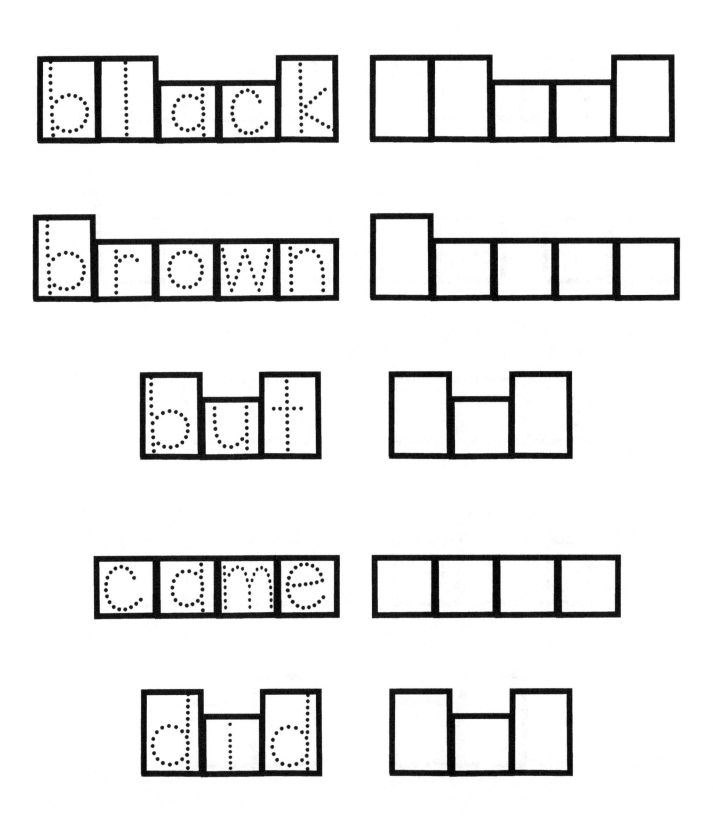

all   are   ate   black   came

am   but   ~~at~~   be   brown   did

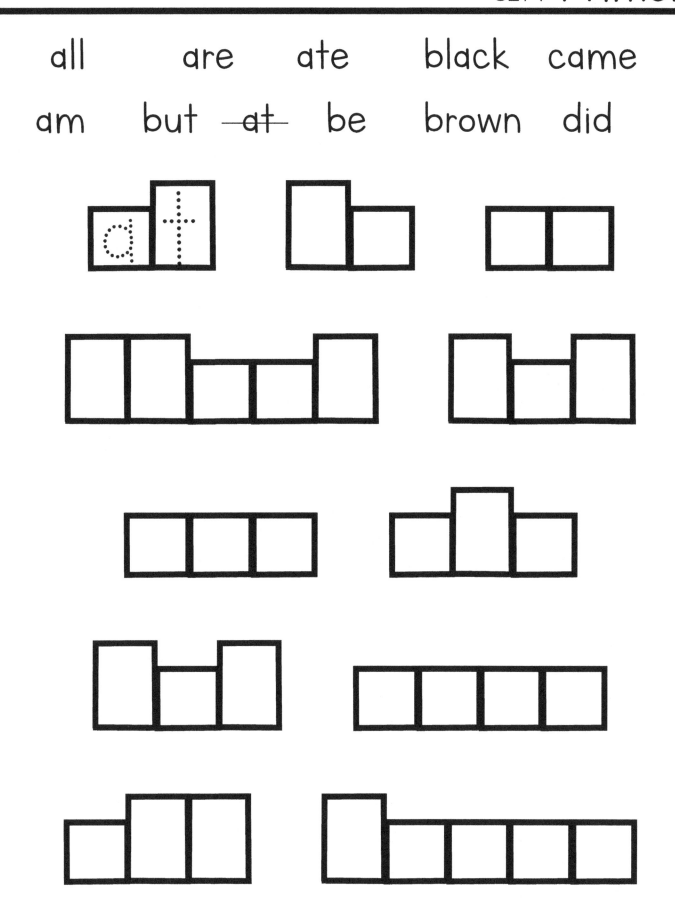

Primer SET 2

h n i (d o) p l i k e

a e n m u s t e a t

v w t h e d p d q y

e y o g p l m j q y

g o o d n j b r q v

f o u r d v g e t z

~~do~~	good	into
eat	have	like
four	he	must
get		new

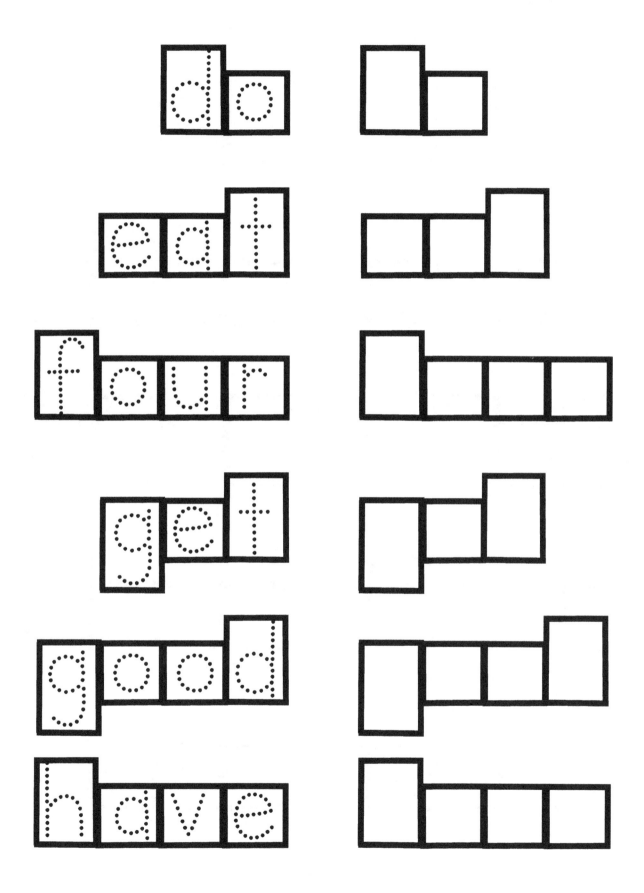

Primer SET 2

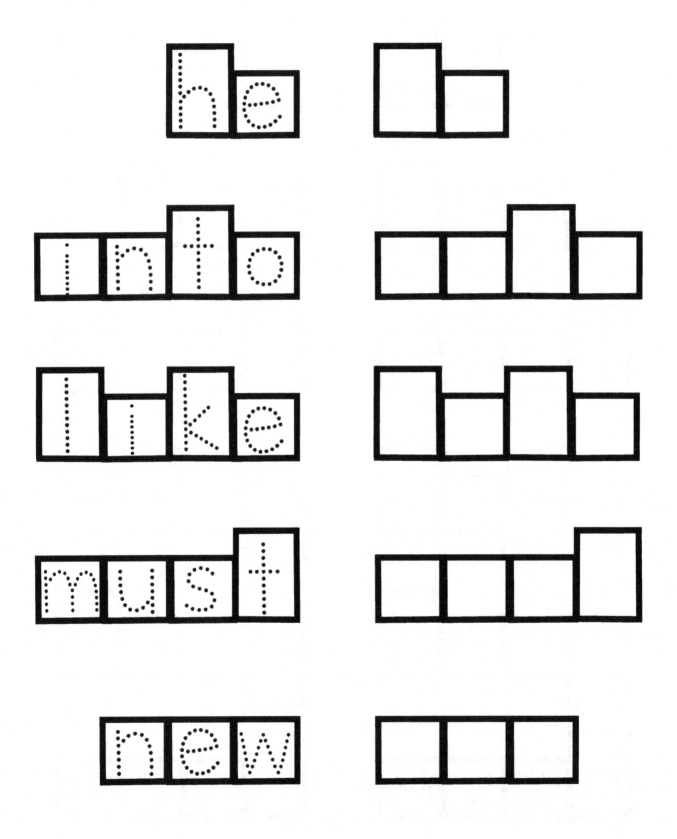

do   four   good   he   into   must
eat   get   have   like   new

Primer SET 3

```
n  r  o  y  t  t  e  r  p
a  n  b  y  g  d  m  d  j
r  t  n  v  i  e  o (n  o)
m  w  d  r  s  j  r  u  t
t  b  x  a  r  n  w  k  t
r  x  e  u  t  o  b  a  m
j  l  o  k  g  w  p  m  s
p  g  n  m  b  g  l  t  d
```

~~no~~	our	ran
now	out	ride
on	please	saw
	pretty	

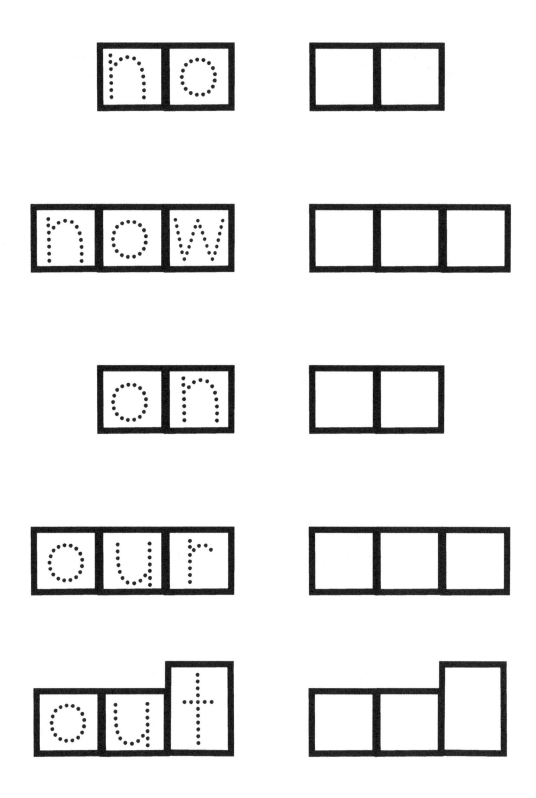

Primer SET 3

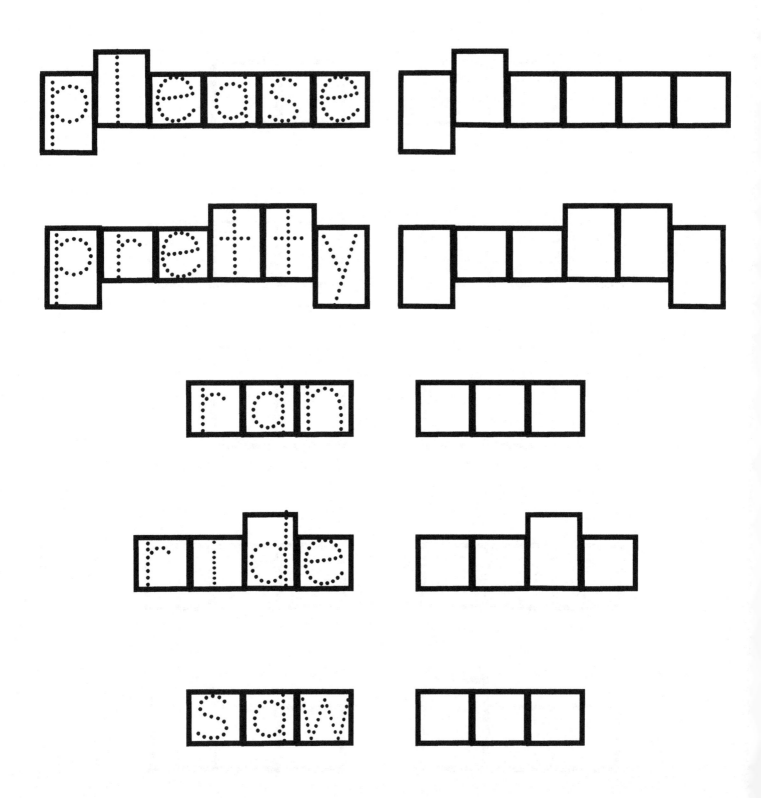

no   ~~on~~   out   pretty   ride

now   our   please   ran   saw

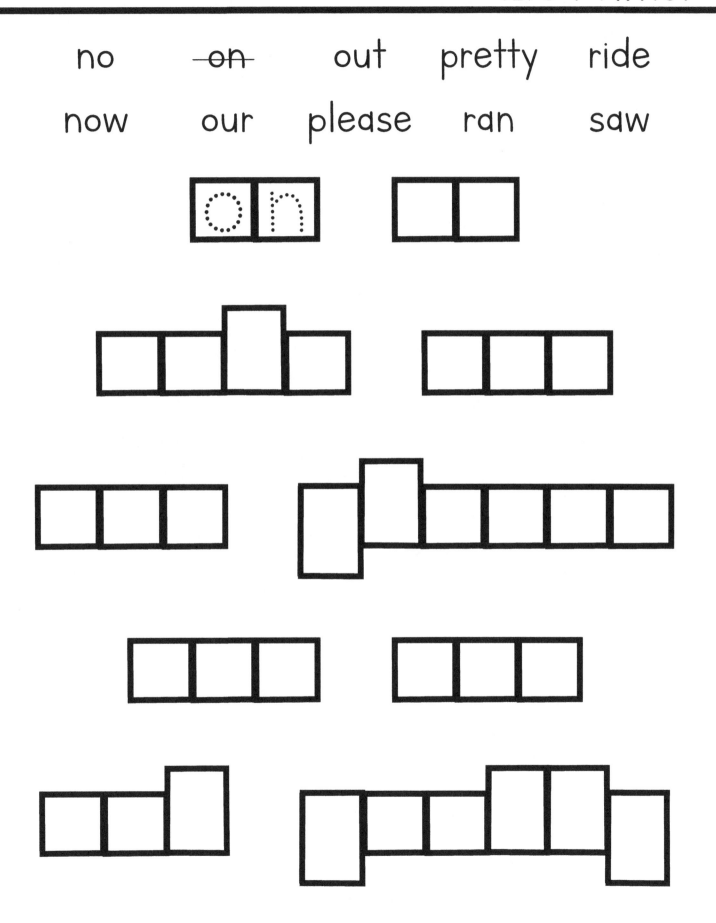

Primer SET 4

```
e  s  b  j  j  w  q  v  d
r  r  a  q  g  y  e  j  l
e  m  e  y  e  h  n  j  v
d  n  t  h  s  b  y  p  w
n  o  t  h  t  k  r  b  y
u  o  o  o  a  s  i  h  t
m  s  o  s  j  t  t  j  r
```

~~say~~	soon	this
she	that	too
so	there	under
	they	

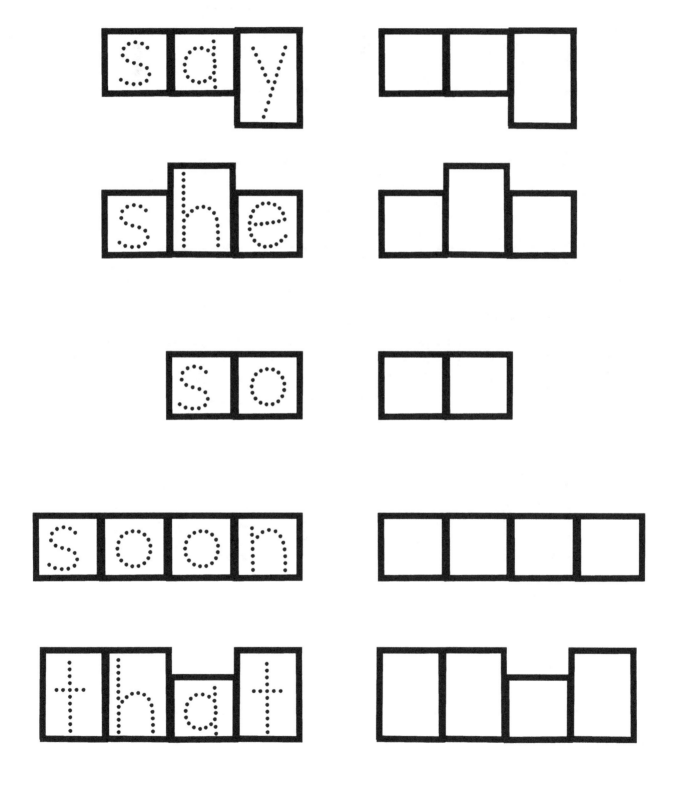

Primer SET 4

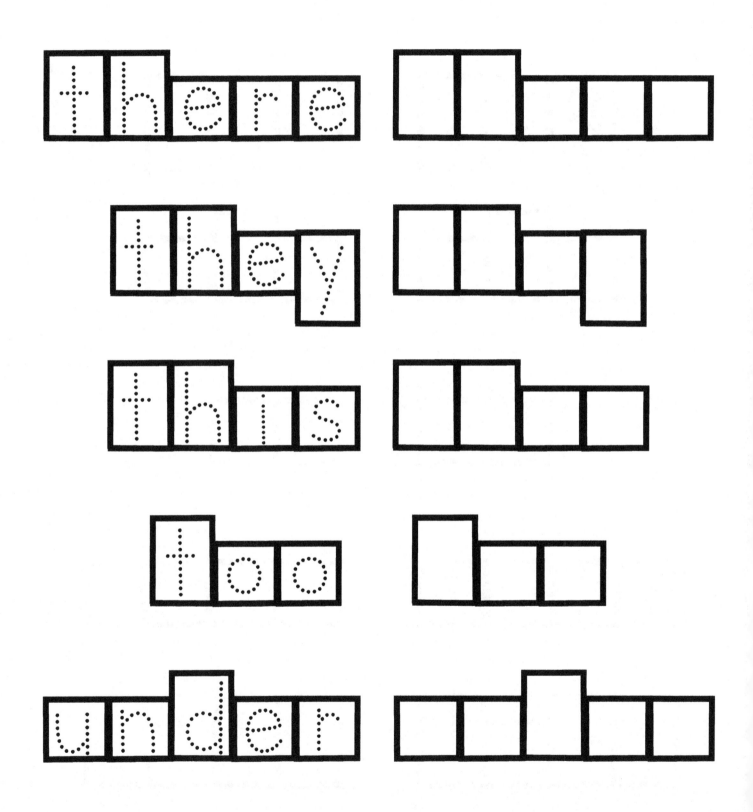

say	so	that	they	too
she	soon	there	~~this~~	under

q l w w w d w

t h a i e h y

o n l w i l z

t l e t i t l

m y e w a t s

y y e h r a h

p t w s w x t

~~want~~   went   will

was   what   with

well   white   yes

who

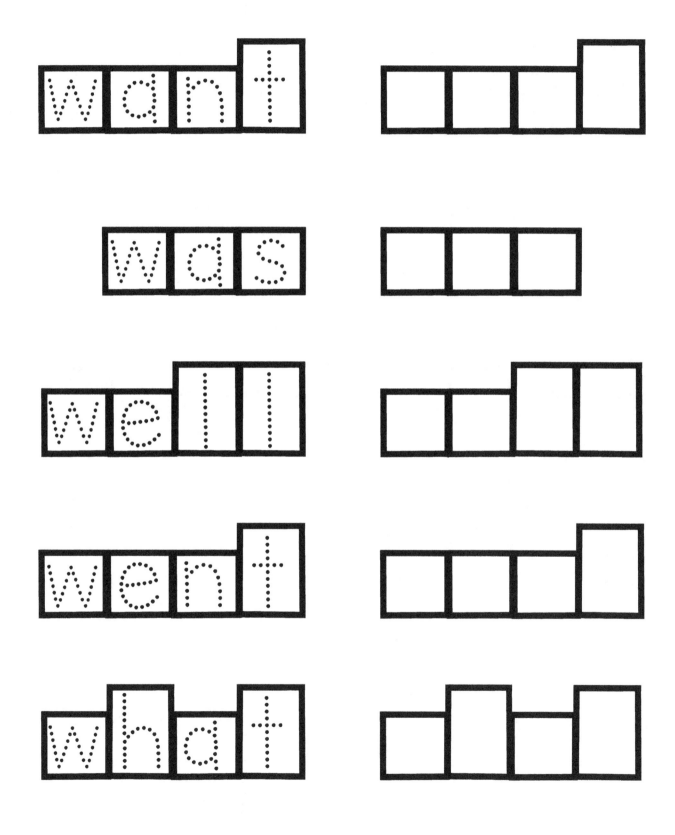

Primer SET 5

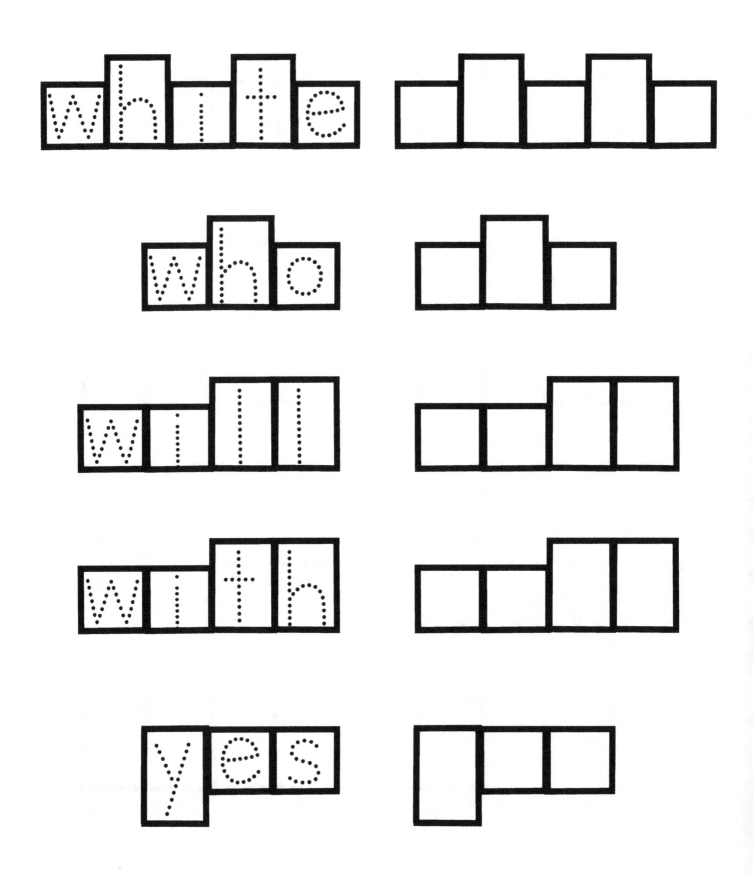

want ~~well~~ what who with

was went white will yes

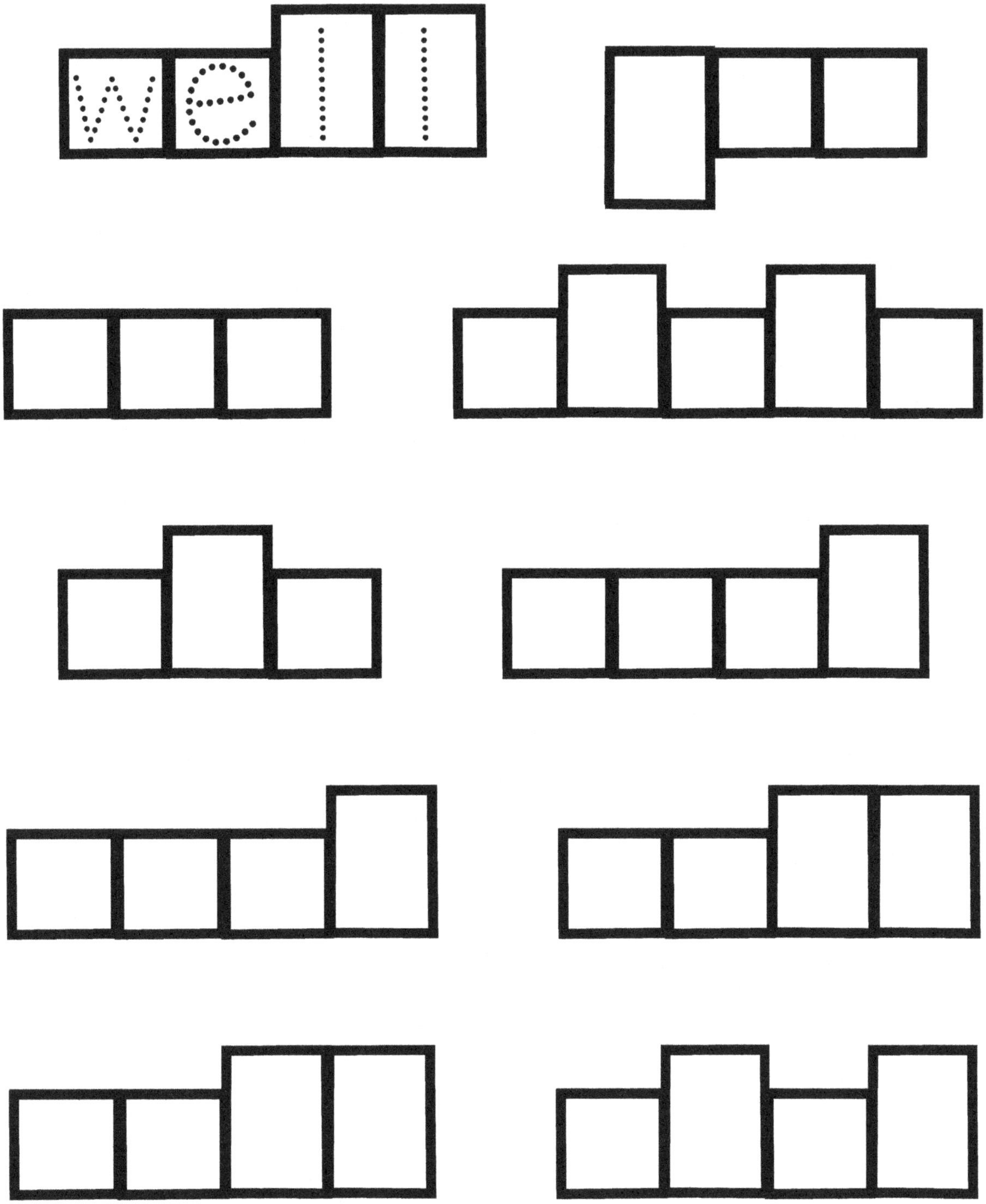

Like Freebies?

EMAIL US AT:

CaterpillarCurlBooks@gmail.com

Write "Sight Word Book" in the subject line to receive a free gift!

This book was designed by a mother of 4 working out of her home in between snacks and during nap times.

If you loved this book, please go to Amazon and leave a review. It makes a HUGE difference for our family!

If you have concerns or suggestions, please email so we can improve our products.

Did You Know?

We have partnered with a

certified Speech-Language Pathologist

to bring you resources to help develop

phonemic awareness and reading

readiness skills in your children.

SEARCH CATERPILLAR CURL ON
AMAZON TO LEARN MORE OR EMAIL US!

Made in the USA
Monee, IL
23 September 2020